THE LONG WAY HOME

THE LONG WAY HOME

LIFELONG LEARNER'S GUIDE TO AUTHENTICITY AND TRANSFORMATION

RACHEL A. RICCOBONO

NEW DEGREE PRESS

COPYRIGHT © 2021 RACHEL A. RICCOBONO

THE LONG WAY HOME

Lifelong Learner's Guide to Authenticity and Transformation

ISBN   978-1-63730-824-0   *Paperback*
         978-1-63730-886-8   *Kindle Ebook*
         978-1-63730-964-3   *Ebook*

EPIGRAPH

———

*"It's a funny thing coming home. Nothing changes.
Everything looks the same, feels the same, even smells
the same. You realize what's changed, is you."*

—ERIC ROTH

DEDICATION

———

For the fighters,
May you continue to walk through the flames
with grace and beauty.

In Loving Memory of:

Sarah Geraghty Kerrane (1911–1996)

Patrick Joseph Kerrane, Jr. (1937–2019)

Eric Lewis Shuhandler (1967–2010)

Armando Riccobono (1936–2007)

Kathleen Harrington Kelliher (1962–2019)

CONTENTS

INTRODUCTION

The ocean has a funny way of bringing things to the surface.

What is it about salty ocean air and crashing waves that makes one contemplate their entire existence? Is it the beauty and peace within the chaos? The ebb and flow of a cascading contradiction right before our eyes? Maybe it triggers our inner child, forcing us to search within ourselves with such a curiosity that acknowledges no bounds.

Often, as humans, we find ourselves stuck and simply surviving within the everyday hustle and bustle. Eventually, the daily stress takes a toll, each frustration taxing our patience. Despite our best efforts, we get swept up in the riptide. Disrupted and disoriented, we fight to come up for air, refusing to let the weight of the world crush our spirit and derail our plans.

Maybe life is meant to be disruptive and unpredictable, though?

Maybe, just maybe... it's not about the highs and lows, but how we allow the unpredictable ride of a lifetime to affect us.

> "The universe is an ocean upon which we are the waves. While some decide to surf, others venture to dive."

—CHARBEL TADROS

Would it be safer to keep our feet buried in the sand, safe and sound from the unpredictable nature of the current? Of course, it would. Yet, the continuous cannon of waves lure us in like a siren call. The splash of salt water, the warm sunshine, and the unexplainable calmness keep us coming back for more. *What's the worst that could happen*, we ask ourselves. No matter how many times those waves knock us down, we get back up, each fumble making us more equipped for the next.

This ride of a lifetime may not be what you wanted, nor what you expected, but it's guaranteed to be a catalyst to your growth. You can coast out into the tide, hell, maybe even get lost at sea—but eventually, you will find your way back home.

> "You can have more than one home. You can carry your roots with you and decide where they will grow."

—HENNING MANKELL

It was on a Thursday evening around seven o'clock when I finally admitted to myself I was lost or simply coasting through life. I was a college sophomore whose hopes and expectations had gone out the window twelve months prior. I had spent the past year coasting down-shit-creek-without-a-paddle. Everything that could have gone wrong went wrong. I lost the contagious love, passion, motivation, and direction I once had. I had crawled into a dark, desolate hole that I was unsure how to get myself out of. I consistently felt defeated and helpless, which were both foreign and out of character for me. I sat, knees to my chest, on a beach nowhere near my college campus as the warm sun set around me. Soft shades of pink, orange, purple, and blue often put my mind at ease and helped me clear my head. The gentle sound of waves crashing often carried away my fear and self-doubt. I felt most at peace and more in touch with myself with my toes buried in the sand.

In the midst of my life crumbling like sandcastles around me, I discovered an influential quote from one of my favorite authors, F. Scott Fitzgerald. I would periodically read these words when I felt lost and confused. They brought me hope, hope that someday I'd get that fierce passion, determination, and direction back in my life. It gave me hope that one day, it would all make sense again. Later down the road, I had this quote printed on the back of my phone case as a daily reminder to myself.

"For what it's worth: It's never too late or, in my case, too early to be whoever you want to be. There's no time limit, stop whenever you want. You can change or stay the same, there are no rules to this thing. We can make the best or the worst of it. I hope you make the best of it. And I hope you see things that startle you. I hope you feel things you never felt before. I hope you meet people with a different point of view. I hope you live a life you're proud of. If you find that you're not, I hope you have the courage to start all over again."

—F. SCOTT FITZGERALD

For those of you who are only familiar with F. Scott Fitzgerald due to his most notable work, *The Great Gatsby*, allow me to take a moment and enlighten you. Francis Scott Key Fitzgerald was an only child born into an Irish-Catholic family, with a wild imagination and undeniable drive for success. His mother came from a wealthy family of wholesale grocers in Minnesota, while his father made a living selling furniture (Biography, 2020). He attended Princeton University, at least until he fell in love and failed out of college. He later joined the United States Army, where he became a second lieutenant in the infantry (Biography, 2020). While stationed in Montgomery, Alabama, he met a woman named Zelda Sayre, the daughter of a well-known Supreme Court Judge. Shortly after, he fell madly in love with Zelda and published his first book, *This Side of Paradise*. Although F. Scott Fitzgerald found great success and fame, nothing in his life truly went according to plan. He continuously found himself starting over, taking a different path, or redirecting his efforts. F. Scott Fitzgerald's work truly encompassed not only the beauty but the ugliness of truth and reality. He had a talent for romanticizing and capturing that dysfunctional reality through his mastery of words.

ABOUT ME

Before I continue, allow me to properly introduce myself. I'm not your average twenty-something, nor am I your typical, entitled zillennial. I'm a dreamer, writer, dancer, sister, daughter, friend, roommate, and lover. I'm a walking contradiction. I'm an open book but have chapters strictly kept under lock and key. I'm mature yet still growing and finding my niche in life. I'm an empath with an old soul who's had an overwhelming zest and passion for life from a young age. I'm an eternal optimist working toward balance in all aspects of my life.

Most of my friends would characterize me as the "most compassionate" or "strongest" person they know. I come from a loving family of four, but we have in no way had it "easy." My parents have poured out their blood, sweat, and tears to provide my brother and me with a better life filled with more opportunity and unconditional love than they had. Despite their hard work, I've been no stranger to adversity in my short lifetime thus far.

Five years ago, I was diagnosed with an autoimmune disease called Hashimoto's Thyroiditis. According to the Mayo

Clinic, Hashimoto's is "a condition in which your immune system attacks your thyroid, a small gland at the base of your neck below your Adam's apple" (2021). The thyroid gland is part of your endocrine system, producing hormones that coordinate many of your body's functions (Mayo Clinic, 2021). Unfortunately, most people aren't even aware they have a thyroid, let alone educated on how much it affects your entire body's function.

In my world, every day brings a new obstacle, concern, or discovery. My life is genuinely never boring. My condition went undiagnosed for several years before a doctor finally caught it. In the years leading up to that diagnosis, I had gained well over sixty pounds, stopped sleeping, started losing hair on my head and my eyebrows, along with so many other symptoms. I looked and felt like a completely different person. I consistently felt like I was screaming for help inside of someone else's body. Even after being diagnosed and being put on medications to supplement the thyroid function my body isn't receiving naturally, I go through seasons with my health. I live with a condition that has "no cure," according to western medicine. That is my daily reality. My health and well-being are a daily stressor, regardless of how "healthy" I eat, how much I exercise, and what lifestyle I decide to live.

"Life isn't about waiting for the storm to pass. It's about learning how to dance in the rain."

—VIVIAN GREENE

Although this discovery has brought pain, trauma, and stress, it's also brought answers, healing, and so much positive change into my life. Not only have my priorities and efforts shifted, but so has my mindset. As someone who is naturally too selfless, putting myself, my time, and my needs first has been a constant struggle. Creating boundaries and only choosing what chooses me has been challenging but extremely rewarding. At this point in my life, my health, happiness, and well-being come before anyone else's opinion, want, or expectation. I no longer serve what fails to serve me.

Make no mistake. It took a lot to get to this point. I may have always made my health and well-being a priority, but when that went south, it made me realize everything I wasn't prioritizing. My failing health only led me to further investigate the areas I hadn't been putting effort into. Which, in turn, lead to significant self-discoveries. For most of my life, I allowed others to drain my energy, put me down, speak for me, and attempt to write my story for me. Until finally, I cracked. My health just happened to go down the drain with it.

I eventually felt the weight of my actions. I felt the consequences of not fully choosing myself. I felt the weight of putting myself last as a means to please or keep the peace with others. The truth is, I don't think I whole-heartedly realized this until I was at my lowest. When everything in my world felt like it was upside down, I was the *only* person that could pick myself up and make everything better. Every ounce of responsibility fell on my shoulders.

It's up to me to set boundaries and protect myself, my time, and my energy. It's up to me to prioritize myself, to show myself love and care every day. Actions speak louder than words ever will. If I truly loved myself unconditionally, it was time to start acting like it. My past may be behind me, but my present and future reside in my hands.

> "Life's roughest storms prove the strength of our anchors."
>
> —UNKNOWN

THE ROAD LESS TRAVELED

In today's day and age, the concept of success and how we "should" live our lives is disillusioned. Society not only tells us but conditions us to believe we must know what we want, have a plan, and stick to that plan to achieve our dreams. While there is truth and validity in this philosophy, that's not always how reality unfolds. Some of the most influential and successful people have taken nontraditional routes to their dreams. They've fallen, pieced themselves back together, strayed from the original path, and had to pave their own way in the world. That struggle and dysfunction just aren't always publicized. We focus on the end result without taking the long, grueling journey into account.

> "The expert in anything was once a beginner."
>
> —HELEN HAYES

F. Scott Fitzgerald is only one of so many examples throughout history; an individual who continuously found himself taking alternative paths he'd not previously foreseen. Look at individuals like Steve Jobs, Larry Page, Sergey Brin, or Jeff Bezos.

Steve Jobs studied physics, literature, and poetry at Reed College in Portland, Oregon, before stumbling into the vast world of technology (Bellis, 2019). Steve, and his cofounder Steve Wozniak, later created the technological empire that is Apple, bringing us everything from computers to iPhones that can now do everything except eat, sleep, and breathe for you. If our phones stopped working tomorrow, I think half of the population would have no clue what to do or how to carry on.

Larry Page and Sergey Brin are the dynamic duo that cofounded Google, a search engine that now serves as a second brain for most of today's society. If you don't know the answer, Google probably does. All you have to do is ask! These two individuals actually met in an engineering course at Stanford while pursuing doctorates in Computer Science (Stanford, 2011). What if these two brilliant minds hadn't crossed paths?

Jeff Bezos left his job on Wall Street to design Amazon from his garage at thirty years old, founding the company in 1994 (Biography, 2021). Amazon is now one of the largest and most versatile companies in the world. On average, 206 million people visit Amazon's site a month (Statista, 2021). For some perspective, that is more than twice the population of Germany. In 2020, Amazon generated over $386 billion in net revenue (Statista).

Where would society be if not for individuals who are capable of thinking outside the box and challenging the status quo? Where would we be without individuals who are willing to take risks?

Innovation and exploration are present in every industry thanks to these free-spirited, open-minded individuals. Where would our world be if not for innovators like Thomas Edison, Alexander Graham Bell, Nikola Tesla, Isaac Newton, or Albert Einstein?

All of these bright individuals have two things in common; their out-of-the-box ideas and their courage to pursue them.

"One of the only ways to get out of a tight box is to invent your way out."

—JEFF BEZOS

While history is full of trailblazers with wildly impressive accomplishments, it's important to remember they were all *human.*

These individuals were once lost too. These successful innovators were once utterly confused as to what they were "supposed to do" with their lives. They, too, questioned what their purpose was. It's essential to remember even the most successful people have been where you're standing right now.

Take a minute to remind yourself this:

You have plenty of time. Success and happiness are not a race to be won. This life we're living is a marathon. Take it slow and get creative.

IT'S ALL ABOUT MINDSET

Society uses the term "normal" loosely. What is normal, though? Does it even exist? Or is it another term we've created that's actually unattainable, just like the idea of "perfection"?

There's no "right" or "wrong" way to live your life, yet others make you feel differently. I'm in a transformational period of my life. I'm a twenty-three-year-old who's finishing her bachelor's degree, working, and trying to find her place in the world. In this, I've taken time to clean out all of the ideas and unnecessary pressures society has filled my head with. I've had to cleanse myself of the toxicity that is groupthink.

Life is often treated like one big popularity contest. We all run around, screwing each other over, just to get a brief view of the top. We spend all of our time and effort trying to fit in or rather fulfill someone else's narrative. So much so we forget to write our own. If we stopped giving power to that pretty, popular girl at the top of the social ladder, maybe we'd be too busy writing our own stories to be bothered with what she's doing.

Moral of the story, reader: Stop living a story you didn't even write. Sit down and decide *who you* want to be before you allow others to tell you who you're supposed to be.

> "Change the way you look at things, and
> the things you look at change."

—WAYNE W. DYER

In life, we inherit a blank canvas. It is up to us to decide what to do with it. Sure, there are some rough edges, maybe a scuff or two, but that shouldn't hinder our progress. As human beings, we all come with baggage of different shapes and sizes. Some of us have more setbacks or hurdles to jump over, but we all have a shot if we choose to take it. You have the power to turn that canvas into whatever you want it to be. You can sit and play victim to society, or you can get up and find a way to achieve your goals. Regardless of your background, you are capable of accomplishing the things you desire most in life. All it takes is courage and a change in mindset. If you tell yourself you'll never be able to do something, how can you ever expect to achieve anything?

P.S. That popular girl is exhausted too. The grass isn't greener on the other side. It's green where you water it.

> "The only person you're destined to become
> is the person you decide to be."

—RALPH WALDO EMERSON

THE JOURNEY AHEAD

I don't have the answers to all of life's mysteries and lingering questions, nor will I ever. At the end of the day, we're all human. We're all simply trying to find our way in this big, confusing world. I still have so much to navigate. I'm still evolving and flourishing into the person I desire to be. I'm a continuous work in progress, and that's okay.

It's okay not to know what lies ahead.

If you're someone who is looking to grow, learn and gain more perspective, this is for you.

If you're still figuring out how to become the best, imperfect version of yourself, this is for you. If you're someone who has big dreams and goals but don't know where to begin, this is for you.

This book is for anyone who wants to be a lifelong learner, embracing the messy journey of life as an opportunity to grow as an individual.

The Long Way Home is your personal journey back to yourself. It's a journey of discovering the most authentic, balanced version of you. This book will inspire readers toward bridging the gap between societal pressures and choosing their own path in life. If you're young and still searching for all the answers, allow me to aid you in your long voyage ahead. Let me shed some perspective and insight to help you better navigate those rough waters. If you've been feeling confused, stuck, or lost, let me put your mind at ease and guide you in a better direction.

The Long Way Home will encourage readers to use the passions and talents in their wheelhouse to achieve the things they desire most in life. Use what's already in your toolbox instead of wishing for what somebody else has! This book will offer refreshing insights and lessons to help shift your mindset. There's no limit to how much you can grow as an individual! *The Long Way Home* will stress the importance of topics like curiosity, motivation, trauma, coping, relationships, and so much more.

Trust the process, trust your journey.

"Twenty years from now, you will be more disappointed by the things you didn't do than those you did. So, throw off the bowlines. Sail away from safe harbor. Catch the wind in your sails. Explore. Dream. Discover."

—MARK TWAIN

The water may be rough, the tide may lead you astray, but choose to ride the wave and see where the journey takes you. After all, what do you have to lose?

Bon voyage mes amis!

PART 1:

ADVENTURE IS CALLING

ADVENTURE IS CALLING

"The journey of a thousand miles begins
with one step."

—LAO TZU

From this point forward, it's about choices.

It's all in your hands, reader. You can choose to take this leap
and better yourself, embracing the daring adventure life so
naturally is, or you can turn back, close this book and remain
exactly the way you were; unchanged and unbothered. The
choice is up to you.

Let me ask you a few questions first though:

- Are you still working toward the very best version of
  yourself?
- Is there anything you can improve on?
- Is there anything you can gain a better understanding of?

- Are there things you still have left to learn?
- Can you be a better human being?

If you answered yes to any of those questions, take this journey with me. After all, what do you really have to lose? Is it more than you have to gain?

In this first section, I will cover:

- Current issues in our society, and how they're affecting your life.
- How not to only survive but thrive in this ever-changing, technologically driven world.
- The power of curiosity, and why we should harness it as our superpower.
- Identifying your physiological needs versus your wants and desires.

CHAPTER 1

HOW DID WE GET HERE?

———

"The great paradox of the twenty-first century is that, in this age of powerful technology, the biggest problems we face internationally are problems of the human soul."

—RALPH PETERS

At times, living in 2020 felt like waking up inside an episode of *Black Mirror*. You're instantly distracted, entranced, and manipulated to think and act in ways that may not benefit you before you've even had a second to think for yourself. Between the vast world of advancing technology, artificial intelligence, and data analytics as well as the misuse of media, public information, and propaganda, the average American has no clue what to think or believe on a daily basis. Information is at our fingertips like never before, but *what is truth?*

Who determines what is said to be fact or reality? Just like perspective, isn't the concept of truth and reality relative to the individual?

"He thinks he's got free will, but really, he's trapped in a maze. In a system. All he can do is consume. He's pursued by demons that are probably in his own head."

—COLIN (WILL POULTER), *BLACK MIRROR: BANDERSNATCH* (2018)

Here in the United States, we're guilty. Guilty of allowing the system, along with its corruption and divisive agendas, to groom us. When the world we inhabit becomes too frightening, we then distract ourselves with the shiny toys it so happily provides us. My question to you, reader... when does it stop? When do we draw the line and choose to engage in difficult conversations? When do we, the people, decide to make an effort and piece ourselves back together?

Are you willing to hear a different perspective? Are you ready to compromise?

Or will we just end up eventually killing each other?

Every day the information, pictures, videos, and news we receive on our phones have the power to influence our every behavior, thought, perception, and mood. The environment we live in orbits around this constant feedback loop, a feedback loop that inescapably determines how we view ourselves if we give it the power to. How we view ourselves determines the life we choose to lead. This domino effect is dangerous if not closely monitored. We now live in a world that can produce immediate results in many facets, which means people now expect immediate gratification. Our frame of mind has shifted, yet some realities haven't.

For instance, you can go out and buy a new outfit, get a new haircut, and order groceries delivered right to your front door, but you can't change your mindset overnight. You can't fix bad habits or heal your heart overnight. There's simply not a quick or immediate fix for everything. You may be able to Amazon Prime that Lululemon dupe, but Jeff Bezos can't help you get your shit together. That's a job only you can do and a job that takes time, as well as a whole lot of patience.

The truth is, the world we live in today is so fast-paced and easily accessible that we forget these harsher realities. We forget that in some respects, nothing's changed. We continue to progress, adapt, and evolve as a species, but have we truly *changed*? Different people, different experiences, but history proceeds to repeat itself, and we continue to learn the same lessons time and time again.

"Look around you. Everything changes. Everything on this earth is in a continuous state of evolving, refining, improving, adapting, enhancing, and changing. You were not put on this earth to remain stagnant."

—STEVE MARABOLI

All I ask is that as you evolve, you look outside yourself, take notes, and challenge each other. Study the people around you and those that came before you. Learn life's lessons and teach them to your neighbors, so we can stop hitting the same roadblocks on our way to a happier, more cohesive society.

A HISTORICAL TRIP DOWN MEMORY LANE

So, *How did we get here,* you ask.

Here in the United States, today's society comprises roughly 332 million individuals (Census, 2021). Of this sum, there are primarily five different generational age groups: the silent generation, the baby boomers, Gen X, millennials, and Gen Z (Statista, 2021). In addition to these, the greatest generation, born before 1928, still makes up a small percentage of our population, with a recorded 1.3 million individuals in 2020 (Statista, 2021).

"Few will have the greatness to bend history itself; but each of us can work to change a small portion of events, and in the total; of all those acts will be written the history of this generation."

—ROBERT KENNEDY

To fully grasp the current state we live in, it's vital to understand where we've come from as a civilization. It's essential to be informed and sufficiently understand how humans have evolved individually and as a mass. How do we differ from our parents or grandparents? What can we learn from each other? As a species, we are continually feeding off each other for knowledge and understanding. Each generation is a building block or foundation for the next to create upon. We should not only look in the mirror at ourselves but toward our neighbors. We might just uncover something new or gain a greater perspective.

Disclaimer: It's nearly impossible to summarize millions of people in a few thousand words. There are entire books written dissecting generational studies. I will do my best to address impacts, trends, traits, and overwhelming narratives as a means to portray how mindset and the idea of success have transformed over the years.

THE SILENTS: SURVIVING WITHIN THE CHAOS

"Is it possible to paint a portrait of an entire generation?"

—TIME MAGAZINE, 1951

The silent generation is a generation of people born from 1928 to 1945, according to the Pew Research Center in Washington, DC (2015). This age group was initially named the "silent generation" by *TIME* magazine. In 1951, *TIME* published a piece discussing the cohort, describing the generation as "a still, small flame; waiting for the hand of fate to fall on its shoulders." Today, there are approximately twenty-one million silents living in the US (Statista, 2021).

Forbes described this group as "children of crisis," coming into the world during a time of great depression, world war, and social unrest (Howe, 2014). This undoubtedly had an impact on their personal journey through life, whether they realized it or not. Sociocultural and historical impacts during one's lifetime have a more considerable influence than we often recognize or give tribute to. With economic devastation, political instability, and domestic hardship came fear, extreme conformity, and survivalist mindsets. This generation was to be seen and not heard. Obedience and respect were the expectations. Instead of striving to change the system, they made the most of working within it (Howe, 2014). For the most part, society conditioned these people to go with the grain rather than oppose the status quo, which one could argue was primarily due to the postcrisis, postwar era they grew up in. The magnitude of such an unprecedented era certainly has the power to steer the direction one takes in life. If your world always feels upside down or inconsistent, you crave stability, right? Even in a perfect world, security and stability pack more punch than we account for when it comes to decision-making.

Given this, it should come as no surprise that in 1965, by the time this cohort was between the ages of twenty-one and thirty-six, 78 percent of people were reported married (Fry et al. 2018). Only 17 percent of this generation was unmarried at the time, with another 5 percent separated or divorced. Silents not only craved security in their personal life but in their professional pursuits. In an article published by the *Chicago Tribune*, Richard Rothschild explains the group's overriding goal was to climb the corporate ladder, unlike today's college grads that talk of starting their own businesses (1999). It's essential to note higher education wasn't as common or frequently required to enter the workforce during this time. In 1965, only 15 percent of men and 9 percent of women had completed a bachelor's degree or higher (Fry et al., 2018).

The silent generation had higher employment rates than both the greatest generation and baby boomers. However, 88 percent of women weren't in the workforce, and the average age they had children was younger than every other generation (Buzzfeed, 2017). This generation's encouraged path to success centered more on marriage, family, tradition, and stable work. Silents highly valued financial security and, ironically, have the most in common with Gen Z regarding their formative years, "both growing up within the difficulties and aftermath of economic and political turmoil" (Ascension Lutheran Church, 2018).

Neil Howe and William Strauss, authors and generational experts, explain that generational names typically derive from where a group of people starts, not where they end up (LifecourseCo, 2011). The silents grew up figuratively in a box, conforming to a world that the greatest (GI) generation before them carefully constructed. It was extremely difficult for them to break out of that prison and challenge ideology. We must remember this as our society continues to progress. These people only knew what they had exposure to at the time. The influence from the world around them significantly shaped their formative years, accomplishments, belief systems, and their attitudes. Instead of judging them for their "outdated views," we should seek to understand and have more in-depth conversations to help see eye to eye with one another.

William Manchester, a well-known historian, once described this generation as "withdrawn, cautious, unimaginative, indifferent, and unadventurous" (Stech, 2021). While I think that description is a bit harsh, I would say silents were traditional, loyal, and hardworking, if nothing else. They had the grit, determination, and a learned strength some of the later generations within American history fall short of. They were not just obedient. They were adaptable. This generation, some of which were born before the invention of the chocolate chip cookie, have experienced everything from the introduction of the microwave to a complete technological revolution. They've had to adapt, transform, and continuously learn as society ran full speed ahead toward innovation and progress. There's something to be said for that type of resilience.

The silents may have spent a great portion of their life walking on eggshells and keeping up with the Joneses, but they also survived through some of the most unprecedented times in American history. Their tentative yet gentle nature may have been a blessing in disguise in some regards.

It is not the strongest of the species that survives, nor the most intelligent that survives. It is the one that is the most adaptable to change, that lives within the means available, and works cooperatively against common threats.

—CHARLES DARWIN

Not everyone born during this time was timid and passive. Individuals such as Martin Luther King Jr., Ruth Bader Ginsburg, and Cesar Chavez were born into this cohort. While the United States has never seen a sitting president from this generation, there are plenty of noteworthy silents that made waves and paved the way for peers and future generations thereafter. They became architects of change, even if it wasn't until much later into their lives.

"One of the great liabilities of history is that all too many people fail to remain awake through great periods of social change. Every society has its protectors of the status quo and its fraternities of the indifferent who are notorious for sleeping through revolutions. Today, our very survival depends on our ability to stay awake, to adjust to new ideas, to remain vigilant, and to face the challenge of change."

—MARTIN LUTHER KING, JR.

BABY BOOMERS: TOO FRIGHTENED TO STOP MOVING

"If you live long enough, you'll make mistakes. But if you learn from them, you'll be a better person. It's how you handle adversity, not how it affects you. The main thing is never quit, never quit, never quit."

—BILL CLINTON

Nine months after WWII ended, "the cry of the baby was heard across the land" (History, 2010). Baby boomers are a generation of people born between 1946 and 1964 (Pew, 2008). The term "baby boomer" derives from the dramatic increase in birth rates following the silent generation and WWII (*Psychology Today*, 2016). Historians believe this dramatic increase may have been due to an overwhelming desire for normalcy after sixteen years of depression and war (History, 2010). Others considered this boom to be a part of a cold war campaign to outnumber communists. The 2020 Census concluded there are now an estimated seventy-three million baby boomers in the United States (2019).

Baby boomers witnessed everything from MLK's March on Washington to Watergate during their formative years. This group has also been referred to as the "flower power generation" due to their pivotal roles within the Civil Rights Movement, Woodstock, and the Vietnam War (Ryback, 2016). With elders still apprehensive, afraid to rock the boat, and pushing conformity during their youth, it's no surprise that eventually, as boomers got older, they either embraced or resisted the consumerist suburban agenda (History, 2010). Some began to rebel against a system that was no longer working in their favor. Boomers fought for social, economic, and political equality. Forbes claims, "baby boomers changed the world, ended a war, created a new culture of values and morphed our style and politics with every move of the Beatles" (Zogby, 2009). Their experiences not only shaped their beliefs and attitudes, but their concept of success and how life should be lived. So much so that their elders eventually followed behind them.

"Throughout history, protests, concerts, and wars have defined generations—baby boomers are no different."

—FRANK OLITO (INSIDER, 2020)

Variations and trends among this generation changed significantly in comparison to their elders. By 1985, 22 percent of men and 20 percent of women had received bachelor's degrees or higher (Fry et al., 2018). As higher education became more widely accepted, military recruits rapidly decreased. Compared to the silents (47 percent) at the same age, only 15 percent of boomers had reached veteran status by 1985. Similarly, the marital status dropped from 78 percent to 56 percent in boomers between the ages of twenty-one and thirty-six (Fry et al., 2018). However, the average age women got married dropped from twenty-two to twenty. There was still an overwhelming societal pressure for women to settle down, start a family, and embrace the roles of mother and wife, a phenomenon which Betty Friedan later coined as "the Feminine Mystique" (History, 1963). By the mid-1950s, the nation began to experience economic comfort and prosperity, giving rise to the middle class. Consumer products began to take off, and so did corporate America. Corporations grew larger and more families moved to suburbia.

Given, not all baby boomers have taken the same route to success. Some separated from the pack, relished in failure, and took risks to see greatness. This generation is known for some of the world's greatest icons. Freddie Mercury, Prince, Tom Hanks, Michael Jordan, and so many more belong to this age cohort. We've now seen a total of four US presidents that are baby boomers. Some boomers went climbing the ladder for financial security like their parents, and others went to extreme measures to rewrite their narrative or be noticed within society. The late Princess of Wales, Diana Spencer, was a boomer with a rebel heart. Her activism, compassion, and glamour made her an international icon. One who's still celebrated over two decades after her tragic death and will be for generations to come.

"It's also possible that the seeds of the boomers' discontent were planted long ago—back when they were young, and their generation reveled in the culture of youth."

—PEW RESEARCH CENTER, 2008

Although I don't believe an entire generation can be fully categorized, I believe it's important to look at overwhelming trends within a group of people. Within this age cohort, there is an overwhelming trend in traits, characteristics, values, and beliefs. While this generation is said to be self-reliant, competitive, goal-centric, and well-disciplined, they are also said to be workaholics (Barge, 2019). Even though they have a stronger work ethic than other age groups, they also tend to have extreme tendencies and pessimistic views. According to the Pew Research Center, this generation has not only reported a lower quality of life, but they are more likely to worry about their income, despite having the highest recorded incomes of any age group (2008). One could associate this group with stress or high functioning anxiety toward their personal finances, or rather money in general, despite being some of the highest earners in American history. Given, this generation of boomers has had not only children but at least one living parent to worry about providing for (Pew, 2008). This has led many baby boomers to develop more pessimistic views toward life and the system they operate in, believing that it's harder to make progress than before and easier to fall behind (Pew, 2008).

Boomers undoubtedly transformed America and the labor force that operates it, but was it for the better?

GEN X: SMELLS LIKE TEAM SPIRIT AND FALSE CHARACTERIZATION

"It is impossible to live without failing at something unless you live so cautiously that you might as well not have lived at all—in which case, you fail by default."

—J.K. ROWLING

Squeezed between two vast, overpowering generations lies Gen X. Often characterized as a lost middle child, this generation of people were born between 1965 to 1980 (Pew, 2020). Last year, there were approximately sixty-five million people in the United States born within this age group (Statista, 2020).

From *Roe v. Wade* to the fall of the Berlin Wall, this generation got lost in the confusion. They are frequently placed in the shadow of baby boomers when they are immensely different and intriguing on their own. Yet, over the years, they've received a bad rap, being referred to by *TIME* magazine as a generation with "few heroes, no anthems, and no style to call their own" (Gross & Scott, 1990). They've also been called baby busters, slackers, thirteeners, and the back to basics bunch. Gen Xers were born during a time of "drugs, divorce, and economic strain" (Gross & Scott, 1990). Their parents raised them to be self-sufficient, hence the nickname "latch-key kids." As they grew older, they felt plagued by the social issues that surrounded them. They felt as though they'd inherited racial strife, homelessness, AIDS, fractured families, and federal deficits from their "self-centered and impractical" boomer parents. Naturally, boomers shared disinterest and disdain, claiming Gen Xers would "rather hike the Himalayas" than dare to climb the corporate ladders they and their parents before did (Gross & Scott, 1990).

While they may not have been as rebellious and outspoken as their parents, Gen Xers embraced their conditioned independence. They reveled in delayed gratification and the notion that "less is more." In *TIME*'s article (1990), a woman described her fellow peers as the "world's carpenters and janitors," claiming they weren't trying to change things but were simply working to fix the system and clean up its broken pieces. One could say this is admirable. They didn't wish to completely uproot the systems in place but dedicated themselves to transforming it with what they had.

While their disdain and lack of respect for their authority didn't earn them colorful reviews, this generation was hardworking and entrepreneurial, if nothing else. By 2000, these adult Gen Xers had a reported median household income of $70,000 (Fry et al., 2018). Higher education continued to rise, with 24 percent of men and 28 percent of women obtaining a bachelor's degree or higher by 2001 (Fry et al., 2018). This is the first time this country had more educated women than men in their early adulthood. Not only that, but 72 percent of women occupied the labor force. Marital status decreased again in this generation. Given, this cohort was born during the "greatest anti-child phase in modern American history" (FutureNow, 2019). With the invention of birth control, the skyrocket in divorce rates, and the large migration of women into the workforce—did we expect this generation to settle down in the burbs like the generations before them? Unlikely. Their independent nature followed them in their personal and professional pursuits.

"The most important thing is to try and inspire people so that they can be great in whatever they want to do."

—KOBE BRYANT

MILLENNIALS: DIVERSE, EDUCATED, AND DISAPPOINTED

Millennials are the group of people born from 1981 to 1996, according to the Pew Research Center (2020). In the United States, there are approximately seventy-two million people (Statista, 2020). Millennials might just be one of the most interesting age cohorts to discuss due to the amount of research done on them.

Most millennials were between the ages of five and twenty when the twin towers were hit, and terror shook our nation

(Dimock, 2019). From the Columbine Shooting to wars in Iraq and Afghanistan, the formative years of this age group were defined by terror and intense political polarization. However, this group can also be defined by technology. The millennials came up in an era of internet explosion.

"Millennials, and the generations that follow, are shaping technology. This generation has grown up with computing in the palm of their hands. They are more socially and globally connected through mobile internet devices than any prior generation. And they don't question; they just learn."

—BRAD D. SMITH

In 2013, millennials finally received their *TIME* magazine cover story debut. However, I'm sure it didn't sit well. *TIME* described this generation as "entitled, lazy, over-confident, tech-savvy, coddled, narcissistic, and a bit delusional" (Sanburn, 2013). Delightful, right? This cohort has frequently been referred to as "the me me me generation." *TIME* went further to assert that "millennials received so many participation trophies growing up that 40 percent of them think they should be promoted every two years—regardless of performance" (Sanburn, 2013). While many argue that millennials are entitled, others argue they're simply adapting quickly to a world undergoing such rapid technological advances. Additionally, it's argued that while they can be over-confident, they're optimistic and pragmatic in their ways, which can be beneficial qualities… "even if it means they spend too much time on their phones" (Sanburn, 2013).

"Every generation brings something new to the workplace, and millennials are no exception. As a group, they tend to be highly educated, love to learn, and grew up with the internet and digital tools in a way that can be highly useful when leveraged properly."

—KATHRYN MINSHEW

The millennials' paths to "success" look much different from previous generations. In 2017, 36 percent of women and 29 percent of men had obtained a bachelor's degree or higher. Although they had the highest record of men (79 percent) and women (71 percent) in the labor force in that same year, they entered the workforce following the economic recession and stock market crash in 2008 (Fry et al., 2018). As many millennials graduated at the height of this economic crisis, they were left with high levels of student loans and fewer job prospects (Kurt, 2020). In a special done by NBC News, they deem millennials the "unluckiest generation in modern history," capturing their resentment and lasting impact from this time in their life (2020). Despite their economic strife, millennials are highly educated and, ironically, the largest generation in the labor force today. One-in-three American labor force participants (35 percent) are millennials (Fry, 2018).

"Gone is the day where you work at a job for thirty years and retire. Millennial jump around and switch careers. I think it's important for CEOs to highlight career mobility within a company so that employees don't get bored and continue to be stimulated."

—KABIR SEHGAL

GEN Z: ANXIOUS DIGITAL NOMADS

"Gen Z represents an unprecedented group of innovation and entrepreneurship."

—GREGG L. WITT, THE GEN Z FREQUENCY: HOW BRANDS TUNE IN AND BUILD CREDIBILITY

Today's youth fall under "Generation Z," born from 1997 to 2012 (Dimock, 2019). Some also refer to this cohort as the "postmillennials" or the "iGeneration." As we're witnessing the formative years of this age group, we have the least amount of research or data to analyze fully. However, here's what we do know!

In 2020, there were approximately sixty-seven million Gen Z in the United States (Statista). Much like millennials, their formative years have consisted of terrorism, social media, as well as cultural and political transformation. This age group doesn't recall a time when the US "war on terror" didn't exist, when same-sex marriages were not legal, or when the national economy wasn't struggling. While only 14 percent of US adults had internet access in 1995, by 2014, 87 percent had access (Parker & Igieknik, 2020). These children don't know a time where technology didn't rule day-to-day function and operation. Gen Z is not only the largest generation but the most racially and ethnically diverse in American history, compromising approximately 27 percent of the US population (Meola, 2021).

In an article released last year by Pew Research Center, Kim Parker and Ruth Igieknik explain how this new generation was in line to inherit a strong economy and record-low unemployment, but due to COVID-19, that's all changed. This unprecedented time has reshaped the country's social, political, and economic landscape, leaving Gen Z with an uncertain future (Parker & Igieknik, 2020). Despite this uncertain future, projections show they will be the most well-educated generation to date.

"In an era of fake news, and the filter bubble, [Gen Z is] also more likely to be able to push through the noise… Not only are they able to consume more information than any group before, but they have also become accustomed to cutting through it. They are perhaps the most brand-critical, bullshit-repellent, questioning group around and will call out any behavior they dislike on social media. (Little wonder brands are quaking in their boots.)"

—LUCIE GREENE

Side Note:

It's important to note that if you're born on the cusp of a generation, it's easy to feel like you portray traits and trends of two cohorts. Truthfully, I didn't know whether I was a part of millennials or Gen Z until doing this research. Even so, I don't feel I quite fit the mold of either, but a fusion of the two. I consider myself what some would call a "zillennial."

NO MAN IS AN ISLAND: BUILDING STRENGTH ONE GENERATION AT A TIME

"We must learn to live together as brothers or perish together as fools."

—MARTIN LUTHER KING, JR.

Every person and every story is unique, but often the finer details connect our journeys.

When we're young, we see things with fresh eyes and a pure heart, questioning everything our elders and ancestors before us have built. It's human nature to think we could have done it better. Maybe we could have? As we age, gaining more maturity and wisdom, it's crucial to recognize how history unfolds and why; the cause and effects of it all. Progress doesn't happen overnight, and as much as we want it to, it never comes fast enough. Yet, throwing history out the window or blaming one another for our missteps along the way will never produce long-term solutions or cohesion. Cancel culture merely leaves us blind and more vulnerable to repeat what others have already uncovered.

Authors have written entire books on these generations of human life. This spark-notes-version of generations throughout the last century of American history doesn't even begin to do each of these groups justice, nor generational groups in other areas of the world. It does, however, stress the importance of perception and understanding.

The ability to put yourself in another's shoes; to understand, acknowledge, and empathize with their experiences may very well have the power to change the world. I believe that with everything I have.

Today and each day forward, I hope you choose to thank and appreciate your elders. I hope you ask them questions, and they tell you lengthy stories in return. Elders, I hope you choose to encourage and nourish the inquisitive and passionate nature of youth. I hope you're able to see things through their eyes, to better navigate your personal landscape as the world around us rapidly changes. I hope you share your comprehensive insights, and they share their new-wave visions with you. I hope you're able to see each other's dreams for the future of mankind.

This life can be cruel and will always be unfair, but it is all we have.

Let's navigate it together.

Be gentle and adaptable like a silent.
Be passionate and disruptive like a boomer.
Be considerate and hardworking like a Gen Xer.
Be confident and optimistic like a millennial.
and Be "bullshit-repellent" like a Gen Z.

"Make up your mind that no matter what comes your way, no matter how difficult, no matter how unfair, you will do more than simply survive. You will thrive in spite of it."

—JOEL OSTEEN

CHAPTER 2

SURVIVING THE TWENTY-FIRST CENTURY

"Here's to the crazy ones. The misfits. The rebels. The trouble-makers. The round pegs in the square holes. The ones who see things differently. They're not fond of rules. And they have no respect for the status quo. You can quote them, disagree with them, glorify or vilify them. About the only thing you can't do is ignore them. Because they change things. They push the human race forward. And while some may see them as the crazy ones, we see genius. Because the people who are crazy enough to think they can change the world are the ones who do."

—STEVE JOBS

My father is a man of grit and survival. He's the kind of individual that could spend all day watching *Man vs. Wild* or *How It's Made*. He's also a man of curiosity.

Whether it's carefully dissecting every Led Zeppelin song or diving deep into historical conspiracies, the man has a wealth of knowledge. One that I always aspired to possess. He seeks to understand the physical world around him better so that when and if the time comes, he's more equipped to withstand the battle. From a young age, I learned to ask the hard questions and be firm in my beliefs, always open to learning but never conforming to the propaganda surrounding me. Like his father before him, he taught me to stand up for what I believe in and never go down without a fight.

As I got older, my abnormal breadth of knowledge and round peg ideas weren't always appreciated or widely accepted. It's easy to vilify people for thinking and seeing things differently than you but let me ask you this:

Why are you so scared of opposition?

It's similar to the concept of relational boundaries that we'll discuss in a later chapter. When people lash out and become angered by the boundaries you set to protect yourself, it's typically because your lack of boundaries benefits them. In this case, are we scared of the rebels or simply further vilifying them because their opposition fails to serve the brainwashed narrative that society is pushing?

Genuinely contemplate that and then get back to me. Aren't they simply seeing things you don't? If nothing else, wouldn't it benefit to hear their side first rather than silence or cancel them?

"We are not supposed to all be the same, feel the same, think the same, and believe the same. The key to continued expansion of our Universe lies in diversity, not in conformity and coercion. Conventionality is the death of creation."

—ANTHON ST. MAARTEN

With what has transpired over the last two years in the US, one would believe our carefully constructed democratic republic is being invaded by socialists and communists alike, who favor groupthink. Groupthink can be defined as a pattern of thought characterized by self-deception, forced manufacture of consent, and conformity to group values and ethics (Merriam-Webster, 2021). Depending on the setting, groupthink can be dangerous and produce irrational decisions.

Consequences of Groupthink may include: (Cherry, 2020)

- Blindness to potentially negative outcomes
- Lack of preparation to deal with negative outcomes
- Failure to listen to differing opinions
- Lack of creativity
- Ignoring important information
- Inability to see alternative solutions
- Overconfidence in decisions
- Resistance to new information or ideas
- Obedience to authority without question

It's frightening to see grown, educated adults falling into traps left and right. I urge you to ask questions and problem-solve for yourself before you turn to the group's findings.

What if that contingency plan doesn't work? What if what they're telling you isn't true? Are you going to go down with the ship or find an open porthole?

The choice is yours. Hope you packed a flotation device!

"For it is dangerous to attach oneself to the crowd in front, and so long as each one of us is more willing to trust another than to judge for himself, we never show any judgment in the matter of living, but always a blind trust, and a mistake that has been passed on from hand to hand finally involves us and works our destruction. It is the example of other people that is our undoing; let us merely separate ourselves from the crowd, and we shall be made whole."

—SENECA (LUCIUS ANNAEUS SENECA)

OUR SOCIAL DILEMMA: IS SILICON VALLEY TURNING US INTO ADDICTS?

"If something is a tool, it genuinely is just sitting there waiting patiently. If something is not a tool, it's demanding things from you. It's seducing you. It's manipulating you. It wants things from you. And we've moved away from having a tools-based technology environment to an addiction- and manipulation-based tech environment. Social media isn't a tool that's just waiting to be used. It has its own goals and its own means of pursuing them by using your psychology against you."

—THE SOCIAL DILEMMA (2020), NETFLIX DOCUMENTARY

For those who have an iPhone, have you ever looked at your weekly screen time? It's easy to scroll aimlessly and not realize hours have gone by. What feels like twenty minutes can quickly turn into two hours of scrolling through different social media apps. The cell phone has gone from a device solely used for communication to a portable computer that comfortably fits into your pocket and manages your entire existence. It has more power and influence over your mental health, decisions, and productivity in your day-to-day life than you may realize. It's eating up our time, our energy, and our brain cells.

We hear the term "Big Tech" tossed around a lot lately. Who is Big Tech, though? And what influence do they have? Big Tech is a term used to describe companies like Apple, Facebook, Google, Amazon, and often Microsoft. These companies dominate their perspective sectors within technology. From internet services to e-commerce, these powerhouses are shaping the way society progresses. We're becoming utterly dependent on their services, which has significantly transformed our economy and society as a whole. These beneficial services and technological innovations have consequences, though.

I didn't get my first phone until sixth grade, and even then, it didn't have a quarter of the capabilities now at children's fingertips. While this progress has its victories, it may very well be "eroding the social fabric of how society works" (Netflix, 2020).

TRISTAN HARRIS: DESIGN ETHICIST OR PSYCHOLOGICAL GENIUS?

"Technology steers what two billion people are thinking and believing every day. It's possibly the largest source of influence over two billion people's thoughts that has ever been created. Religions and governments don't have that much influence over people's daily thoughts."

—TRISTAN HARRIS

Tristan Harris is President and cocreator of the Center for Humane Technology. Tristan was recently in a documentary on Netflix called *The Social Dilemma* (2020), which reached thirty-eight million viewers in the first four weeks of debuting. The Atlantic magazine deemed him the "closest thing Silicon Valley has to a conscience" (2020). After studying Computer Science and Human-Computer Interaction (HCI) at Stanford, Tristan became a Design Ethicist and Product Philosopher for Google. It was there that he grew concerned about how ethically and morally irresponsible tech was progressing.

The Netflix documentary includes insights from various former founders, creators, and technical pioneers of the platforms our world revolves around today, in addition to experts in social psychology, human evolution, and much more. All of which express ethical concerns about how these services we rely on aren't being used in the manner they were intended to be. They collectively give their expertise and experiences at companies like Twitter, Facebook, Instagram, etc., stressing that the business and goal of all these social media platforms is to *win your attention*. These trillion-dollar companies are profiting from our insecurities, addictions, and identity crises. If we were to stop consuming their online services, they'd stop making money. From surveillance capitalism to artificial intelligence and manipulative algorithms, it's frightening how much data and control these platforms have. Yet, we happily swipe, refresh, and spend every waking hour consuming. Tristan Harris compares social media apps to Vegas slot machines, exposing the psychological framework behind the design and operation of these apps.

Tristan, and others in his field, are taking strides toward changing the way we design, use, and progress with technology moving forward. The mission of the Center for Human Technology is to "reframe the insidious effects of persuasive technology, expose the runaway systems beneath, and deepen the capacity of global decision-makers and everyday leaders to take wise action" (Center for Human Technology, 2021).

For anyone who hasn't seen the documentary or looked into the insights of individuals like Tim Kendall, Jeff Seibert, Shoshana Zuboff, or Justin Rosenstein—I encourage you to do your research. These are pressing issues that affect our world, our collective conscience, and how we operate daily. Technology and social media are shaping our youth, feeding them groupthink and instant gratification.

"We're all vulnerable to social approval. The need to belong, to be approved or appreciated by our peers, is among the highest human motivations. But now our social approval is in the hands of tech companies."

—TRISTAN HARRIS

DISTRACTIONS: IDENTIFY AND LIMIT

"The problem is that technology has become an extra limb for some of us. It's important to utilize this technology, but at the same time, it's important to know when to take a break from it."

—ALEX BROCHES, START LIVING...NOW!

We live in a world where there are so many distractions and external forces competing for our attention, time, and effort, pulling us away from not only ourselves but from what actually matters at the end of the day.

Who will you give your precious attention to, reader? Social media, school, work, friends... who's going to win?

We live in a digital age. Our world revolves around one thing: the internet. The internet never sleeps. We live in a time where work and play intersect, where we're online or available more than we're not, and where we're constantly tied to one handheld object. Your phone that runs off an internet connection plans for you, thinks for you, and even provides you validation. We wake up, and before we even raise our heads off the pillow, we check our phones for notifications. We wake up and immediately crave the "dopamine hit" that our phone, and the applications on it, so happily provide.

In this technological advance, we've lost touch with the physical world. We're so busy building a virtual identity that we lose touch with ourselves and the world around us. Have you ever turned your phone off, taken a road trip or maybe even a short hike, and just disconnected for a while? How did it feel? Did you feel more connected and in tune with yourself, your thoughts, and your emotions? When we eliminate some of these demanding forces in our life, we're able to grow and expand. Silencing social media, public opinion, and social standards are necessary from time to time. I'm not saying to banish it altogether, but you need moments of clarity to truly flourish without distraction or blatant manipulation. Surrendering to such daily distractions can be debilitating to your personal growth and development. Your time is precious.

"One of the problems of modern society, or the post-internet age, is that there are so many things bombarding us that we could care about. I think it's more important than ever to really get clear and focus on what's worth caring about and what's just noise or distraction."

—MARK MANSON

Identify the distractions in your everyday life and make an effort to limit them. We live in a time where we have to set boundaries with the people in our lives, as well as the technological devices we operate. Like anything else, it's about finding balance. Use technology and other tools to your advantage, aiding your growth and productivity, but also know when it's time to put those things to the side. Know when to put your phone or laptop down and reconnect with the physical world.

Set up times where you *digitally detox*. Whether this is a few hours in the evening near dinner and bedtime or on the weekends, find time to be entirely off-line. Cater it to your schedule and preferences, but make time to be more present. Try using the do not disturb function, turning on airplane mode, or even putting the phone in another room; out of sight, out of mind.

FROM COOKIE-CUTTER TO NO MAN'S LAND

"What is cookie-cutter," you may ask? This is an unoriginal and lackluster way of thinking that is socialized into our young minds from an early age. We're force fed the ole American Dream; told we must play by the rules, always do the right thing, and in most cases, go to college to find a job that pays enough to support a family and adequate lifestyle. We're taught that higher education is the golden ticket to financial freedom and a happy life. Is this still true, though?

While higher education has become increasingly popular over the years, I'm not sure what narrow-minded human being decided this route was "the only way" or "the right way" to success. Allow me to shed some light.

As the cost of higher education rises and certain degrees become obsolete, is it really worth it? For some, yes. For others, no. That's the simple answer, folks. Sure, are individuals with college degrees most often higher earners? Yes, but not always. What about trades and arts? Not everyone can be a doctor, engineer, or computer programmer. The world needs construction workers, service professionals, and electricians. We live in a world where an average person can go from invisible to viral internet sensation overnight. The possibilities are endless, and the world around us is changing each and every day. Do your research and choose something that's not only going to pay the bills but make you happy. That doesn't always have to include the all-American college extravaganza.

"You don't have to be a genius or a visionary or even a college graduate to be successful. You just need a framework and a dream."

—MICHAEL DELL

I've spent my entire life passionate yet overwhelmed. Always questioning which "path" I should take in life. Society, and maybe even the household I grew up in, has conditioned me to think and feel like I had to choose a predetermined, preplanned path to succeed. For a long time, I did. "Follow the steps that other successful people already have," my family and mentors would say. Don't get me wrong, this has validity and comes from a loving place. Your parents want to see you succeed. They want to help you succeed in the easiest way possible. If it worked for them, it should work for you, right?

Yet, what if you find yourself struggling along their pre-carved path? Sometimes, we must turn to the road less traveled; some of us need to fail and struggle to find what's best for our individual goals and needs.

Can't I be successful by exploring the unknown and finding my own way? Isn't this what successful people had to do before society thought for us?

Don't successful and innovative people think for themselves?

For someone like myself, who is curious, multifaceted, and open-minded, there are an endless number of routes or paths I could see myself taking, all of which would make me happy as a clam. So, why should I try to plan out my *entire* life?

Instead, why can't I embrace my gifts, give time and effort to my passions, and see where life takes me? Of course, I can still have plans, create short—and long-term goals, and be strategic in how I want to achieve success, but why does it have to be concretely predetermined? Am I not allowed to stray from the blueprint here and there?

Why does society place a *due date* on knowing exactly what you want?

Whether it is your career, your relationship, or your happiness, give yourself time. Take the time you need to comprehensively process without feeling the pressure of others around you.

ENOUGH IS ENOUGH

As I sit here, a twenty-three-year-old college grad still figuring out life, I've repeatedly asked myself the same questions:

"Who am I to be writing a book when I don't have it all figured out?"

"How can I advise and help others if I am still striving to find balance too?"

Society has made me think that I have to be "put together," certain, and perfect (whatever the hell that is) at any given moment. Society has consistently made me question whether I am good enough, giving me a hefty dose of impostor syndrome. Merriam-Webster would define impostor syndrome as a false and sometimes crippling belief that one's successes are the product of luck or fraud rather than skill. This is the phenomenon of feeling like we're faking it, when in all actuality—we're probably killing it.

According to *TIME* magazine, over 70 percent of people experience the feeling of impostor syndrome at some point in their lives (2018).

Stop giving into this toxic thinking. You do not have to have it all figured out. You do not have to be put together. You're allowed to be a hot mess with no clue where your life will head. This doesn't make you a failure! You're allowed to give yourself time to figure things out. **There's no due date for your dreams. There's no due date for success. And there is certainly no due date for happiness. Take your time. The world can wait.**

I went from being the most imaginative, playful, carefree child to a perfectionist who worries about everything imaginable. Now, at a time where my creativity and artistry get put to the test, I've consistently felt crippled with impostor syndrome. With every step I take, the quicksand of self-doubt and societal pressure tries to pull me into its depths.

I won't give in to the pressure. I won't categorize my thoughts and ideas into someone else's mold. My thoughts, ideas, and feelings are my own.

If you take nothing else out of this, please remember:

- It is *okay* not to have everything figured out.
- It is *okay* not to know where you're going.
- It is *okay* to not yet know what you want, need, and deserve.
- It is *okay* not to be *okay*.

- It is *okay* to be a work in progress.
- It is *okay* to be afraid of the unknown.
- It is *okay* to change your mind.
- It is *okay* to change course and take your life in a different direction.
- It is *okay* to be confused.
- it is *okay* to take your time.

"Behind every successful man, there's a lot of unsuccessful years."

—BOB BROWN

MOVING FORWARD: THE PATH YOU CHOOSE FOR YOURSELF

"Eighty percent of success is showing up."

—WOODY ALLEN

Ultimately, this is your life, reader. I'm just the one narrating it inside that big brain of yours at the moment.

The more I research, ponder, and discover, the more I believe everything in life boils down to one thing: perspective. Success looks different for everyone. So, if I were to give you any advice moving forward, it would be to stop invalidating your own view. Who gives a shit if others can't conceptualize it?

Everyone and their nosy mother aren't always going to agree with your decisions in life. But you see, that's the beauty. They don't have to. Limit the distractions, discover your vision, and run with it. Small wins are victories, too, you know.

Thanks for showing up today.

CHAPTER 3

STAY CURIOUS

"Yesterday is history. Tomorrow is a mystery. Today is a gift. That's why it's called the present."

—ALICE MORSE EARLE

There's something so special about waking up before the sun rises. As everyone else is sound asleep, you're breathing in the new day. It's as if you know a secret everyone else has yet to discover. So, you smile, letting the cool air brush across your face. You drive a little slower, appreciating your surroundings and the mysterious gift you've received. Each day that we wake up and draw breath is truly a blessing. But we are never guaranteed tomorrow. So, drive slower, smile more, and never take that gift for granted. Today is yours; what will you choose to do with it?

"I hope you realize that every day is a fresh start for you. That every sunrise is a new chapter in your life waiting to be written."

—JUANSEN DIZON

When I was an out-of-state student living in San Diego, I did quite a bit of exploring. Whenever I felt stressed, lost, or overwhelmed, I'd hop in my car and just drive, sometimes with no particular destination in sight. Finding a new spot to explore was one of my favorite pastimes. I'd let my curious nature take charge, guiding me wherever my Nissan Sentra would take me. Sometimes my feet would end up walking along a new beach, and other times, I'd land myself in a new pub with cold beer, live music, and phenomenal people watching.

I suppose you could say I'm an adventurer at heart. I went in search of hidden treasures in this new city, but also within myself. Following my curiosity allowed me to discover things I hadn't known about myself. Things that had been buried deep within me for years. That's the funny thing about life. You can walk in circles for years in search of something you knew was there all along. You just never quite knew how to explain, proving not all those who wander are lost. In fact, in the area of personal growth and development, I don't think the majority of us are lost. Most of us are just uncomfortable with change. At first, it's scary to brave the unknown, but when we finally do—it triggers the exploratory senses of our inner child, shining a flashlight to every corner until we have a firm understanding. Transformation is meant to be difficult, uncomfortable, and maybe even a little bit scary. Falling into the unknown, entering new chapters of life, and not knowing what lies ahead is naturally frightening. However, it should also be thrilling. You're exactly where you're supposed to be. Be curious and let your heart lead the way.

"Be fearless in the pursuit of what sets your soul on fire."

—JENNIFER LEE, CHIEF CREATIVE DIRECTOR

OF WALT DISNEY ANIMATION STUDIOS

THE POWER OF CURIOSITY

"The art and science of asking questions is the source of all knowledge."

—THOMAS BERGER

On average, four-year-olds ask about 300 questions a day. Research also shows by the time these same children reach middle school, they're asking near zero questions each day (TED, 2018).
What causes us to stop asking questions, though?

Where does our curiosity go?

In 2018, Spencer Harrison and Jon Cohen gave a TEDx Talk about why curiosity is our superpower and how society, as well as some organizations, stifle that curiosity. Jon Cohen is currently the Chief Research Officer at SurveyMonkey, and Spencer Harrison is an Associate Professor of Organizational Behavior at INSEAD.

Harrison and Cohen explain that as we grow older, we start to ask more pragmatic, procedural questions. As children travel through our education system, this socialized machine strips them of their curiosity and exploratory senses by training them to limit their interest to practical concerns. The system conditions their primary focus to be on what their superiors want or expect from them.

So, "what enables someone to stay curious?"

Spencer Harrison talks about their extensive research to find an answer to this daunting question. After reading countless autobiographies of Nobel Prize winners, they started to discover a commonality among them. Many of these creators describe a moment in their life when someone else "authorized their curiosity, and it became a part of their identity." This could be a parent, a teacher, or even an organization, but once this becomes a part of one's identity, we allow or give ourselves permission to think outside the box. We allow ourselves to explore the unknown without the limitations society places on us. When we identify with being "curious," we allow ourselves to ask "why." When another person accepts and validates our curiosity, we allow ourselves to do the same. It's only then when we allow ourselves to claim it as our own.

"If we worked on the assumption that what is accepted as true really is true, then there would be little hope for advance."

—ORVILLE WRIGHT

BORN CURIOUS OR RAISED CURIOUS?

So, I suppose my next question to you is, are we born curious or raised to be curious? Or is it a little bit of both?

"We were lucky enough to grow up in an environment where there was always much encouragement to children to pursue intellectual interests; to investigate whatever aroused curiosity."

—ORVILLE WRIGHT

Orville and Wilbur Wright are considered the "forefathers of flight" (Smithsonian, 2021). In 1903, these two American inventors and pioneers of aviation piloted the very first engine-powered airplane in history (History, 2020). Where would travel and transportation be without their limitless curiosity?

While their accomplishments weren't at first celebrated, their legacy lives on. The Dayton, Ohio duo didn't receive a formal education, but their passions and inquisitive nature were encouraged and nurtured. Through experimentation, trial, and error, they were able to achieve greatness.

Much like the Wright brothers, I grew up in an environment and around loved ones who embraced my curiosity and creative pursuits. In fact, I don't believe I'd be the woman writing this book if they hadn't. Although being curious and passionate about so many different niches has been quite the obstacle as I've grown older, it's also been the greatest gift. I can't help but be thankful for the encouragement I received. Curiosity has been a catalyst in my personal growth.

Similar to the Wright brothers and other examples throughout history, my curiosity was authorized by those around me, allowing me to harness those skills. That curiosity then became a part of my identity. I was always encouraged to be not only curious and creative but well-rounded, and I believe it's served me well. I may be indecisive at times due to having more than one desired path to go down, but there's a part of me that enjoys the options. I know I'll land on my feet no matter which door I choose to open. Even if I fail at first, I have the drive, determination, and curiosity to excel in whatever my heart desires.

WHY CHOOSE CURIOSITY?

"Remember to look up at the stars and not down at your feet. Try to make sense of what you see and wonder about what makes the universe exist. Be curious."

—STEPHEN HAWKING

I spend a lot of my spare time pondering, trying to make sense of the universe we've found ourselves in. Dear friends of mine can testify, as only a rare few can whole-heartedly keep up and engage in these long-winded, philosophical conversations with me.

We live in a world full of wonder, mystery, and endless possibilities. We live in a world full of contradiction and opposition. A world overflowing with diversity. One man's trash is another's treasure. What one man views as beautiful, another views as ugly. Everything is relative. Perspective is indeed in the eye of the beholder. The systems, beliefs, inventions, and institutions of the society and world we live in are a result of curiosity and exploration.

Without curiosity, how are people supposed to progress?

How can we evolve as a species without forward-thinking?

The mysteries of life are no different from the uncharted territory within each of us. When we take the time to understand ourselves better, we are able to understand, empathize, and relate to those around us.

Curiosity is, in fact, our superpower as human beings. Curiosity plays a giant role in your personal journey of growth and development. You can set a goal and achieve it, but if you don't have that drive, curiosity, and adventurous side to dig deeper and keep reaching for more, how far can you go?

How much can you actually evolve without curiosity?

"We keep moving forward, opening new doors, and doing new things, because we're curious and curiosity keeps leading us down new paths."

—WALT DISNEY

On December 5, 1901, a visionary was born. Walter Elias Disney was an ordinary man with an extraordinary mind. His childlike wonder, expansive imagination, dedication to progress, and determination for success continue to touch the lives and hearts of those all over the world nearly a century later. Walt embodied the unfiltered curiosity that lives within each of us. He continuously failed and invented new paths for himself. From an early interest in art to efforts in the Red Cross during WWII, multiple failed business ventures, to creating an empire, Walt's curiosity and perseverance kept him striving for more (Britannica, 2021). Nearly ninety years after his creation of the beloved Mickey Mouse, the Walt Disney Company is among the "largest companies in the world by capital marketization" (Statista, 2021). In 2020, the company generated over $65 billion in global revenue. From media networks to theme parks, resorts, consumer products, and studio entertainment, Disney dominates and will continue to for years to come.

"I have no special talent. I am only passionately curious."

—ALBERT EINSTEIN

HOW TO STAY CURIOUS

"The important thing is not to stop questioning. Curiosity has its own reason for existing."

—ALBERT EINSTEIN

We've discussed curiosity as a whole, but what does it mean to "stay curious"? What does that look like?

Bob Borchers is currently the VP of Worldwide Product Marketing for Apple. In 2016, formerly a Chief Marketing Officer for Dolby Laboratories, he gave a TEDx Talk on the power of curiosity. In his talk, he discusses eight habits found in curious people. These habits include:

1. They listen without judgment.
2. They ask lots of questions.
3. They seek surprise.
4. They're fully present.
5. They're willing to be wrong.
6. They make time for curiosity.
7. They aren't afraid to say, "I don't know."
8. They don't let past hurts affect their future.

These are wonderful insights from Mr. Borchers, some of which I hadn't previously attributed to myself. It's no wonder his professional life sky-rocketed after this talk. Clearly, curiosity has enriched his life too.

Staying curious means banishing your ego as a means to fully assess, explore, and comprehend any given situation. It's accepting there's no possible way you know everything or have a perfect point of view. For me, staying curious means investing time; even if it's five minutes a day, I make time to research, read, or investigate a subject that fascinates me. Whether it be diving deep into historical rabbit holes or within myself, I make time to nurture my curiosity, as it can be an influential tool in my personal, professional, and social life.

SELF-DISCOVERY: SEARCHING FOR BURIED TREASURE

"Knowing yourself is the beginning of all wisdom."

—ARISTOTLE

Inside each of us is a little explorer, philosopher, or scientist, persistently asking questions, testing, and forming hypotheses about our mental, physical, and emotional state.

The process of acquiring insight into one's own character is the definition of self-discovery. Although this concept is simple in theory, the act of discovering one's true self can be perplexing. Some people go their entire life without truly discovering who they are. This process requires both curiosity and exploration, and you can achieve this through self-reflection.

According to the University of St. Augustine (2020), self-reflection can have the following benefits:

- Develop emotional intelligence
- Strengthen your confidence, communication, integrity, and relationships
- Produce sounder decision-making
- Help optimize your skillset

Self-reflection can be exercised through journaling, meditation, or thoughtful contemplation. However you may choose to exercise this, here are some questions to ask yourself:

- Who are you when no one is watching?
- What three words describe you best?
- When and with whom do you feel most like yourself?
- What motivates you?
- What inspires you?

ROAD MAP TO DISCOVERING YOUR TRUE SELF

So how do we discover ourselves? From my experience and the expertise of others, I have compiled a list of ten steps to self-discovery.

STEP 1: BE STILL AND TAKE NOTES.

Sometimes you have to stop, observe, and assess things before moving forward. So much can be learned within observation, and it's often overlooked. Take time to really examine your communication, motives, behaviors, actions, and reactions. Adam Smith (2021), author, entrepreneur, and speaker, explains that often silence scares us but is essential to our growth and understanding of self.

STEP 2: MAKE SENSE OF YOUR PAST.

As you begin this new journey, you must retrace the narrative you're currently writing or glance over the places you've been before you can look ahead to the places you wish to go.

STEP 3: EXPLORE WHO YOU ARE, NOT WHO YOU WANT TO BE.

Be honest with yourself. Notice, I did not say critical. Experts suggest taking personality tests or self-evaluations to aid self-exploration (Smith, 2021). Although these assessments aren't perfect, they're helpful.

STEP 4: INDIVIDUALIZE YOURSELF.

Who are you without anyone else present? How do you view yourself? Acknowledge the things that make you different.

STEP 5: FIND OUT YOUR STRENGTHS AND WEAKNESSES.

Discover what you're good at, but more importantly, what you're not good at.

STEP 6: FIND PASSION AND MEANING.

What makes you abundantly happy? What makes you feel valued or important? Identify things, activities, and areas of your life that provide you with deeper meaning and help you impact the world around you.

STEP 7: OPEN YOUR EYES TO A NEW PERSPECTIVE.

Every individual sees life through a different lens. Ask someone for their perspective on something that's been taking up space in your mind. Be open to opposition and don't take anything too personally. Be open and accepting of feedback. You may learn something new. Be open to seeing things through their eyes.

STEP 8: EVALUATE WHERE YOUR TIME AND EFFORT LIE.

This one is always interesting. Our time and efforts don't always lie where we want them to, but the truth of the matter is *you* are in full control of this. Whether it's a job, a relationship, school, the gym, healthy eating, or maybe even making time to write a book, get up and do it. If it means that much to you, you need to make time for it. Sit down, evaluate all of your responsibilities, and allocate the amount of time and effort you're able and willing to spend on each one. Really be honest with yourself. This is where it comes in handy to know yourself and your habits. Don't create a plan that you know you can't stick to. That will only create more stress for you. Be realistic, but most importantly, have patience with yourself. After all, Rome wasn't built overnight!

STEP 9: CREATE NEW GOALS FOR THE JOURNEY AHEAD.

Creating new goals that align with your current and future wants, needs, and desires is exciting. This is the fun part. Take time to recognize the story you're writing. If you're not happy with it or where it's going, it's never too late to start over. Rewrite your story! Creating these goals is inspiring. Seeing them through is the difficult part. Keep that excitement and hope in your back pocket and let it push you forward. Have patience; the journey ahead isn't short and isn't easy.

STEP 10: PUT YOUR PASSION INTO ACTION!

It's not enough to simply dream. Take action toward things that excite you!

THE JOURNEY AHEAD: ADVICE FROM YOUR PIT CREW

"If there's one thing I've learned in my life, it's that curiosity might kill cats, but it doesn't kill people."

—TRACY MORGAN

Try to convince me otherwise:

The saying "curiosity killed the cat" was invented by people who simply didn't want you to know the answers.

Curiosity is the catalyst to self-actualization, education, innovation, and transformation. It even has the power to engage the brain's circuits for memory and reward, increasing our ability to learn new information (Barclay, 2014).

As you navigate your personal journey, I encourage you to seek advice and wisdom from those around you but also to discover things for yourself. I encourage you to ask questions and investigate the things that fascinate you.

There's no such thing as a stupid question, reader. Throw out the pragmatic framework someone taught you. Ask away!

"Research is formalized curiosity. It is poking and prying with a purpose."

—ZORA NEALE HURSTON

CHAPTER 4

WHAT YOU WANT VERSUS WHAT YOU NEED

———

"A musician must make music, an artist must paint, a poet must write, if he is to be ultimately at peace with himself."

—ABRAHAM MASLOW

Our wants and needs frequently compete in a tug of war with each other. We're constantly questioning what we should do, even though instinctively we know we have needs to meet.

How many times have you gone out with your girlfriends and sacrificed your sleep? Or ordered greasy take-out because you were craving it, but know you have healthy groceries in the fridge that you have to cook? There are so many scenarios I could play out here, but you get the point.

How many times have you sacrificed what you need for *what you want*?

In the madness of everyday life as ambitious human beings, we often mistake our wants and desires for our *needs*. We get so wrapped up in our own dysfunction that these lines become blurred, but the truth is these are very different entities. Often, we focus more on our wants and desires rather than what we actually need to function as humans, resulting in self-neglect or poor self-care.

"You always know. You have basic needs, and when they aren't met, your body sends signals. Hunger, loneliness, exhaustion, thirst, and fear are all signals that something is missing, and you need to act on it now."

—MEL ROBBINS

Think about the last time you had to meet a deadline or had a hectic week at work. Now I want you to answer the following questions:

- How much sleep did you get that week? Were they quality hours?
- Did you properly fuel your body with food? Was it nutritious, or did you gravitate to whatever was easily available?
- Were you stressed? Did you feel this affected your mental and emotional health?

Much like the musician, the artist, and the poet—we place our desires above our physiological needs. It is true that an artist must paint, and a musician must make music if they are to be truly happy, but if they don't eat or sleep, they can't do anything. We must serve the vessel we occupy first so we can deliver those talents. Everything else is secondary. Our mental, emotional, and physical well-being should be our number one priority each day. That deadline doesn't matter if you can't breathe! Putting our physiological needs first is of the utmost importance, as well as being able to distinguish these among our wants and desires.

MASLOW'S HIERARCHY: IDENTIFYING AND PRIORITIZING YOUR PHYSIOLOGICAL NEEDS

"To the man who only has a hammer, everything he encounters begins to look like a nail."

—ABRAHAM MASLOW

Abraham Maslow identified a set of biological requirements called *physiological needs*. His motivational theory, called the Hierarchy of Needs, was developed in 1943. This theory emphasizes the principle that, in a means of human survival, one's biological needs must be met before any other secondary needs can be fulfilled. These primary needs include air, food, sleep, shelter, etc. Once we find equilibrium within these lower-level needs, we can fulfill higher-level needs like love and belonging, self-esteem, and self-actualization.

Why are these needs important to our survival? And how can we successfully regain balance with them?

"YOU ARE WHAT YOU EAT."

"Our food should be our medicine, and our medicine should be our food."

—HIPPOCRATES

We live in a world that is constantly circulating and obsessing over the latest trends. Diet is no exception to this. Like any other area of life, we search for convenience rather than taking the time to nourish our bodies with the healthiest options. We're all guilty, constantly seeking a quick fix. Whether it's a drunken excursion to Whataburger or a bag of Doritos on your short lunch break—it's not cutting the mustard, kid.

When we sacrifice our nutrition for convenient consumer goods, we're sacrificing our health. According to the CDC (2021), those who adopt healthy eating patterns live longer and are at lower risk for serious health complications. A balanced diet can help prevent heart disease, diabetes, hypertension, high cholesterol, autoimmune diseases, and cancer (ProHealthCare, 2017).

"You're made of elements. Take the time to learn the foods with high element properties in order to save your health and your body."

—DR. SEBI

Adopting practices like avoiding processed foods and eating more plant-based foods can significantly improve our overall health (ProHealthCare, 2017). Instead of immediately turning to Weight Watchers, juice cleanses, and fad diets, go back to basics. Aim for a balanced diet of proteins, fats, and carbohydrates. Depending on your activity level, weight, height, and health goals, breakdown in macronutrients looks different for everyone. However, healthy eating doesn't have to be hard.

This year, Healthline released an article outlining twenty-eight health and nutrition tips that are "actually evidence-based" (Gunnars, 2021). Some of these healthy tips include:

- Limiting sugary drinks
- Limit refined carbohydrates
- Feed your gut bacteria
- Use plenty of herbs and spices
- Eat plenty of fruits and vegetables
- Avoid restrictive diets

Moms and boss daddies alike, even optimizing for frozen fruits and veggies is a small win. Typically, this produce is picked and frozen at its peak, when it obtains the most nutrients. Save yourself time in the kitchen.

I've had to transform the way I fuel my body due to my autoimmune disease, but meal prepping and detailing my grocery list is a lifesaver. I'm busy and don't always have the time to make a meal, but prepping these nutrient-rich meals for the week, or even a couple of days at a time, saves me so much stress.

"Water is the most neglected nutrient in your diet, but one of the most vital."

—JULIA CHILD

In addition to our need for food, the human body depends on water to survive. Water is our body's principal chemical component and makes up approximately 50–70 percent of our body weight (Mayo Clinic, 2020).

The US National Academies of Sciences, Engineering, and Medicine determined that an adequate daily fluid intake is:

- About 15.5 cups (3.7 liters) of fluids a day for men
- About 11.5 cups (2.7 liters) of fluids a day for women

Most experts recommend we drink eight glasses of water per day. Mayo Clinic (2020) describes this as a reasonable goal, even though total fluid intake may vary based on exercise, environment, and overall health.

"The doctors of the future will no longer treat the human frame with drugs, but rather will cure and prevent disease with nutrition."

—THOMAS EDISON

While Edison wasn't on par with how American healthcare evolved, there are still doctors who believe in natural healing and practices. I'm no doctor or medical professional by any means, but I've spent a great deal of time researching different foods, herbs, and supplements that may help my condition or my overall health and well-being. If this interests you, I highly recommend reading *This Is Your Brain On Food* by Dr. Uma Naidoo. Dr. Naidoo is a board-certified psychiatrist, nutrition specialist, and professionally trained chef. She argues what we eat affects more than our bodies. It also affects our brain. Her national bestseller uses cutting-edge research to explain the various ways in which food contributes to our mental health.

MOVE YOUR BODY

"Reading is to the mind what exercise is to the body."

—JOSEPH ADDISON

It's not simply enough to eat healthily. We must find equilibrium among all of Maslow's lower-level needs. Maslow may not have included exercise in those needs, but I (as well as science) believe it's crucial to our health and well-being.

According to the Mayo Clinic (2021), regular exercise and physical activity has a range of benefits, including weight control, disease prevention, mood enhancement, energy boosting, promoting better sleep, increased sex drive, and promotes social activity. Much like the power of nutrition, the CDC argues that it also promotes brain health and increases your chances of living longer (2021).

I grew up playing team sports and grew to love physical activity, but as we get older, it's harder to keep up with. Squeezing a gym session into the workday or even a home workout in-between Zoom calls can be tough.

Here are my favorite ways to sneak in more physical activity every day:

1. Walk and Talk

Whether I'm walking aimlessly around a neighborhood or incline walking on the local gym's treadmill, talking makes the time fly by. On days when I don't feel like working out but know I should, I pair it with a task I enjoy doing. Whether this is catching up with my mom, listening to a podcast, or hitting play on my favorite playlist at the moment—It's not hard to get in the zone and get that workout in.

2. Take the Stairs

When given the option of stairs or elevator (given that you're not five minutes late for your meeting), take the damn stairs. Get those steps in!

3. Walk the Dog

Obviously, if you don't have a dog, I can't help you there. However, this can be a fun and stress-relieving experience for you and your cute pup. Another great way to implement physical activity into your busy day!

"Exercise to stimulate, not to annihilate. The world wasn't formed in a day, and neither were we. Set small goals and build upon them."

—LEE HANEY

NOT JUST FOR THE DEAD: SLEEP MORE, WORRY LESS

"Your future depends on your dreams, so go to sleep."

—MESUT BARAZANY

How many of you actually prioritize your sleep? Do you have a regular bedtime?

This has always been a struggle for me. Growing up in a household where my parents never enforced a bedtime became an issue as I got older. I was always that child who perpetually stayed up late and could get up early if needed, fully capable of taking on the day with minimal rest. Same for my teenage years. Not getting home from Friday night football games until the wee hours didn't faze me. I could still get a couple of quality hours and get up for morning cheer practice. Yet, when my health was failing, and I was no longer sleeping consistently... I couldn't function. I've watched the nightfall turn into dawn more times than I can count. I saw the effects and toll it has on my brain and body. Good news, though, folks! You can prevent sleep deprivation.

The National Sleep Foundation (2021), Mayo Clinic (2021), and Harvard Medical School (2019) have all confirmed an average of seven to nine hours of sleep per night is healthy for adults ages eighteen and older. In an article published by Healthline, Watson & Cherney (2020) discuss the harmful effects of sleep deprivation. These negative impacts may include memory issues, mood changes, weakened immunity, weight gain, trouble with thinking and concentration, high blood pressure, low sex drive, and risk of heart disease or diabetes. Poor balance and risk of accident are also possible impacts. Watson and Cherney explain that when we're sleeping, our brains form connections that help us process and remember. Therefore a lack of sleep can negatively impact not only our short and long-term memory but concentration, creativity, and problem-solving skills (2020). Sleep deprivation can lead to anxiety and depression, making us moody, emotional, and quick-tempered (Watson & Cherney, 2020). Yet, I think the most important of these is immunity. Especially during a global pandemic, we must make sure we're implementing daily practices and habits that strengthen our immunity rather than deplete it. Our immune system is a natural superpower that defends us against viruses.

What about *oversleeping*, though?

This is one of those double-edged swords, where you're damned if you don't and damned if you do too much. Johns Hopkins Medicine has claimed that sleeping too much can also be problematic. Oversleeping is associated with type 2 diabetes, heart disease, obesity, depression, headaches, and a greater risk of dying from a medical condition (Johns Hopkins, 2021).

As a means to keep you rested and healthy, here are some habits to implement:

Healthy Sleep Habits to Implement—(Watson & Cherney, 2020)

- Limiting daytime naps (or avoiding all together)
- Refraining from caffeine past noon or at least a few hours before bed
- Avoiding heavy meals within a few hours before bedtime
- Exercise regularly
- Reduce alcohol intake before bedtime
- Keep a consistent sleep schedule, create a routine that works for you
- Turn off electronic devices at least thirty minutes before bedtime
- Spending an hour before bed doing relaxing activities, such as reading, meditating, or taking a bath

GIMME SHELTER: HOME SWEET HOME

"Housing is absolutely essential to human flourishing. Without stable shelter, it all falls apart."

—MATTHEW DESMOND

As of January 2020, my home state of Arizona had an estimated 10,979 people experiencing homelessness. Of this total, 809 were families, 921 were veterans, 633 were unaccompanied young adults (ages eighteen to twenty-four), and 2,086 were individuals experiencing chronic homelessness (USICH, 2020).

According to public school data reported to the Department of Education, there were an estimated 21,062 students that experienced homelessness during the 2018–2019 school year in the state of Arizona (USICH, 2020).

These numbers are alarming, to say the least. This is *one* state, people. Shelter is undoubtedly our most under-appreciated need. Next time you wake up and complain about how long the drive-thru line at Starbucks is, check your privilege. Count your blessings for waking up with a roof over your head.

"I don't want to sound like a Hallmark card, but to be able to wake up each day with food and shelter, that alone is good. Forget aging and the fact that my butt is becoming a little more familiar with my knees than my tailbone. If you are six feet above the ground, it's a good day. So, give me more!"

—FAITH HILL

PSA to all the humanitarian hearts: Change starts at home. We need to combat the issues within our own backyard before we go trying to fix problems that plague the rest of the world.

STAYING AHEAD OF THE GAME

"An ounce of prevention is worth a pound of cure."

—BENJAMIN FRANKLIN

We may not be able to predict the future or change our past, but what we choose to do with the present *matters*. Our health matters. Taking the time to do your research, have conversations, and ask questions about how to take preventive measures is key. Given, sh*t happens. Sometimes, perfectly healthy people experience health complications. However, if you can lower your chances, why wouldn't you? By prioritizing your physiological needs and learning how to be better at meeting them, we can take our health into our own hands.

Educating yourself on the importance of our immune system, the dangers of inflammation, mental health, or even sexual health is pertinent to our growth and overall well-being.

"It doesn't take a brain surgeon… or a cardiologist… or a pediatrician… or even a policy wonk to figure out that a penny's worth of preventive care is worth many dollars of sick care."

—HEIDI MURKOFF

SEXUAL AND REPRODUCTIVE HEALTH: FROM TABOO TO NECESSARY

Riddle me this, reader.

Early psychologists hypothesized that human nature was driven and dictated by our need for pleasure. We procreate new life mostly as the result of such pleasures. Yet, we aren't allowed to talk about it? People aren't uncomfortable engaging in such scandalous activities, but they're taken by surprise when someone formally addresses it. Forget about sex. What about reproductive health? And no, we're not just talking about periods here, people. How did such an important topic become taboo? An educated conversation about the birds and the bees quickly turned into abstinence and scare tactics.

Does anyone remember the alarming version of "sex ed" taught in school? Maybe those of us that went to public school only endured such a traumatic event. Nonetheless, how is scaring a twelve-year-old with pictures of sexually transmitted diseases supposed to teach them how to keep their body healthy and safe? Why wasn't my class of anxious girls engaging in discussion about period tracking, consent, safe sex, hormones, and other helpful habits that contribute to not only the productiveness of my sexual organs but my body's overall function?

"What this means for parents is that you never know what your child's 'sex education' class may entail. Only fourteen states require that sex ed be medically accurate."

—PEGGY ORENSTEIN, GIRLS AND SEX: NAVIGATING THE COMPLICATED NEW LANDSCAPE

Like most boys and girls around the world, I learned about the finer details of sex and sexuality through peers, books, films, and Google. Keep in mind, today's children practically have unlimited access to the internet. That's an even scarier place to turn for answers. The real question here is:

Why aren't these answers coming from educated, caring adults who are responsible for your physical, psychological, and social development?

Why are we shying away from such important conversations?

According to the World Health Organization, "a central aspect of being human throughout life encompasses sex, gender identities and roles, sexual orientation, eroticism, pleasure, intimacy, and reproduction. Sexuality is experienced and expressed in thoughts, fantasies, desires, beliefs, attitudes, values, behaviors, practices, roles, and relationships. While sexuality can include all of these dimensions, not all of them are always experienced or expressed. The interaction of biological, psychological, social, economic, political, cultural, legal, historical, religious and spiritual factors influence sexuality." *(WHO, 2021).*

As stressed in TEDx Talks by Dr. V. Chandra-Mouli and Dr. Olivia Richman, these tough conversations need to happen.

Diminishing the stigma surrounding sexual and reproductive health is essential as we attempt to create a healthier and informed society.

Whether it be educating fathers about their daughter's menstrual cycle, confronting mental health, or informing the public about inflammation's lethal impact on the human body, these discussions are necessary for the greater good.

YOUR HIGHEST SELF: CLIMBING MASLOW'S PYRAMID

"For an author, writing is not a want. It is a need. It might as well be the second level of Maslow's Hierarchy of Needs; right after food, water, and shelter."

—JANELLE ALLUM

Once we meet our physiological or primary needs, we can begin to dive deep into our deepest wants and desires.

Maslow theorized that once we fulfill our survival needs, we need safety, security, love, self-esteem, and self-actualization.

- Safety and Security describes our need for health, employment, property, family, and social stability (Homeless Hub, 2021).
- Love and belonging describe the need to form and maintain friendship, family, and intimacy. Humans are social animals, which has been proven throughout our evolutionary history (Escalante, 2015).
- Esteem can be defined as the need to feel respected. If this higher-order need is lacking, people tend to experience

low self-esteem, an inferiority complex, weakness, help-lessness, and even depression (Escalante, 2015).

- Self-actualization is the highest level of Maslow's pyramid, concerned with the "realization of one's full potential" or desire to accomplish everything we can and become the most one can be" (Escalante, 2015). Hence, how most people attribute meaning to their life.

We will unpack all four of these higher-order needs in greater detail in the coming chapters.

"A flower can't grow without sunshine, and man can't live without love."

—DR. SEBI

PART 2:

FALL SEVEN TIMES, STAND UP EIGHT

PART 2 INTRO:

FALL SEVEN TIMES, STAND UP EIGHT

———

"Success is not final, failure is not fatal: it is the courage to continue that counts."

—WINSTON CHURCHILL

七転び八起き

The saying "fall seven times, stand up eight" is an old Japanese proverb. There have been countless variations over the years, but all versions emphasize the courage and willingness to continue despite our fumbles.

The impact and meaning of this proverb made me think of Winston Churchill and the quote you see above.

There's a common misconception about growth and progress. Reader, I'm here to remind you these things aren't always *linear*. Your growth isn't going to just be an uphill battle. It's going to have twists, turns, and setbacks you won't be able to foresee. Remind yourself you've committed to a journey despite its unpredictable and unforgiving nature.

Although there is light within healing, growing, and learning, there is bound to be darkness. You're going to have bad days. Days that may seem utterly impossible to get through. You're going to have to put on your bravest face and confront your demons. It is not going to be easy. Anything but that, actually.

So, when things get rocky... I want you to remember this proverb.

The battle you're fighting is infinite. It's also a choice. You must wake up each day and choose to put in the work, regardless of how you feel. When life inevitably kicks you down, dust yourself off and *get up.*

In this section, I will cover:

- Creating healthy boundaries and healthy relationships, as well as the importance of self-love and self-care.
- Everything you need to know about trauma and how to cope with it.
- The never-ending struggle to find balance in your life.

Your failures are not fatal, and your success is not final.

Keep getting up. Keep going. Keep growing.

Your biggest cheerleader,
R

CHAPTER 5:

DRAW THE LINE

——

"You cannot pour from an empty cup. Take care of yourself first."

—NORM KELLY

Making yourself a priority can often feel selfish or wrong. Often people tell us that it's dishonorable to think of ourselves before others, but allow me to stop you right there.

Merriam-Webster defines the word selfish as "concerned excessively or exclusively with one's own advantage, pleasure, or well-being without regard for others" (2021). Is this always the case, though? While there is truth to this definition, sometimes one needs to be selfish without regard for others. Excessively? Not so much, but you get the point.

Everything in moderation, folks!

On a personal note, I've always struggled with people-pleasing. Putting my foot down and concerning myself with only my well-being from time to time has saved me. There is nothing selfish about taking care of yourself or showing yourself love. You simply cannot give to others if you do not take the time to fill yourself with love first. Making sure your needs are met first ensures you are capable of meeting others' needs. Protecting your time, efforts, and energy is crucial to your mental, emotional, and physical well-being.

You must simply… *draw the line.*

Starting right now, it's time to start making yourself, your wants, and your needs a top priority. Everyone else comes second to you. The support system of family, friends, and loved ones around you will understand this. If anything, you taking the time to better fulfill your needs will improve and enrich your relationships with them in return. So, choose *you.* Stop exhausting yourself. Life is too short to give, give, give and get less in return.

Choose to fill your cup so that you can pour more love into others.

"Friendship with oneself is all important because without it one cannot be friends with anyone else in the world."

—ELEANOR ROOSEVELT

HOW TO BE SINGLE AND THRIVING

"You alone are enough. You have nothing to prove to anybody."

—MAYA ANGELOU

There is such a stigma about being single. We're socialized to perceive our singleness as an indicator of our worth, but that couldn't be further from the truth. Being single doesn't equate to being unwanted or unworthy. Instead, being single is about taking the time to improve and work on yourself. We must individually put in the work and learn how to meet our own needs to effectively fulfill a future partner's needs. My thoughts go back to our first quote in this chapter. Being single is about learning how to fill your cup; that way, later down the road, you can pour love into yourself *and* others.

DEFINE SINGLE

In an article published by *Psychology Today*, Bella DePaulo, a psychologist at the University of California Santa Barbara, explains how the word "single" is multidimensional. Dr. DePaulo claims there are three different definitions for single, asserting that one can be *legally* single, *socially* single, or *personally* single (2011). Being *legally* single means you are not legally married. Being *socially* single, Dr. DePaulo describes as a state of being in a romantic relationship that other people do not regard as serious (2011). Lastly, being *personally* single is when you categorize yourself as single.

Dr. DePaulo did a TEDx Talk in 2017. At the time, she was sixty-three years old and never married. She gives her audience a deeper look into her lifelong singleness and how she never wanted what everyone else did. "Everything about my life added up to a different story," she explains, describing single as her own happily ever after (2017). This narrative just isn't normalized or encouraged throughout society, or history for that matter. DePaulo has made it her life's mission to discover "the true stories of single life, the stories no one is ever telling us" (TEDx Talks, 2017).

Dr. Bella DePaulo presents three different familiar tales we often hear about relationships:

1. "Married people have someone. They have the one. Single people have no one."
2. "Get married, and you'll never be lonely again."
3. "All you need is love. Love is all you need."

Over the last few decades, research studies have been misleading or fallen short in proving these claims, and DePaulo takes noble pride in debunking the myths. We're fed this "commitment industrial complex" from the top-down, consistently told fairytales of how happy we'll be if we have someone to marry and share our life with. So, we become distracted, fixated, and strive to achieve that special status. In the US alone, over a thousand laws benefit and protect *only* people who are legally married. Socially, professionally, and legally, single people experience different struggles and hardships. Popular culture even frequently depicts singles as insufferable, when in fact, singles may experience "more fulfilling social lives and experience greater psychological growth than some married people" (Benincasa, 2016).

You may not love every aspect of being single, *but* that doesn't mean it doesn't have its own unique benefits.

"There is no one blueprint for the good life. What matters is not what everyone else is doing or what other people think we should be doing, but whether we can find the places, the spaces, and the people that fit who we really are and allow us to live our best lives."

—BELLA DEPAULO (BENINCASA, 2016)

WHY SINGLE: THE BENEFITS OF BEING UNCUFFED

Studies indicate that single people are more likely to have stronger social networks, prioritize their physical health, and experience personal growth throughout their lifespan. Studies also show as we get older, those same social networks and the relationships we build are a strong predictor of health and happiness (Brodwin, 2018).

TIME magazine published an article in 2018 outlining nine ways in which being single could improve one's quality of life (Jalili, 2018). From that list, I'd like to share what I found to be most influential. If nothing else, being single is a chance to become financially independent, make self-care a priority, and learn to enjoy your own company. In the long run, taking time to master these components can significantly improve your quality of life and relationships later down the road. Another brilliant point *TIME* makes is that you're more open to the opportunities that come your way when you're single. Being single allows for the freedom of taking more risks and being more adventurous. Now, this is not to say you can't have all of these things within a relationship. You absolutely can. However, when you're single, you're not additionally accounting for that other person's priorities, needs, and desires. This is the perfect time to take chances, make mistakes, rebuild yourself, and redefine what it is you truly want out of life.

Figuratively, you're the writer and main character of your own story. Act like it!

"I don't need Prince Charming to have my own happy ending."

—KATY PERRY

In 2018, Elite Daily published an article advising singles from relationship experts (Kravitz, 2018). The piece contains recommendations from Alysha Jeney (relationship therapist), Evan Marc Katz (author and dating coach), Julia Bekker (matchmaker and relationship coach), and Bridgette Hall (matchmaker).

These four experts say that singles should:

1. Be Approachable
2. Keep An Open Mind
3. Stress Less
4. Put In Effort
5. Enjoy Your Alone Time

Out of these, I've found the ability to be approachable and keep an open mind to be the most impactful. Forget the hunt for a romantic partner. These two principles apply to everything else in life. Whether it be an unexpected job offer, a kind stranger that turns into a friend, or simply being open to exploring things beyond your comfort zone—these two practices are guaranteed to change your life.

Being single might be one of the most extraordinary times of one's life. You can agree. You're also more than welcome to disagree—but frankly, my dear, I don't give a damn.

Gold stars to anyone who got that cinematic reference.

Whether you're single by choice or perpetually wishing you were coupled up, I hope you choose to see the many benefits and blessings of this chapter in life. Take this time to date yourself! Thank me later.

"Discover why you're important, then refuse to settle for anyone who doesn't completely agree.

—FISHER AMELIE

DANCE TO THE BEAT OF YOUR OWN DRUM

"Every day, you reinvent yourself. You're always in motion. But you decide every day: forward or backward."

—JAMES ALTUCHER

Time to answer the age-old question:

What the f*ck do single people do?

What don't they do? This would be a more reasonable question to ask. Being unclaimed territory doesn't exactly warrant having a free schedule. Ironically, I think I've been historically busier while being single than when in any relationship. When I'm single, it's actually easier to spread myself thin and fill up my calendar without mercy.

Let's discuss this idea of "dating yourself" more, though. When in a relationship, you naturally leave pockets of free time in your schedule in hopes of spending quality time with that special person. In this case, singles should also be penciling in free time, but rather to spend with and on themselves.

According to *Bustle* (2015) and *Cosmopolitan* (2020), here are eight activities to do when you're single.

1. Travel
2. Develop Your Interests
3. Declutter
4. Try New Things
5. Invest in Old Friendships
6. Expand Your Circle
7. Reinvent Yourself
8. Sketch Out Future Plans

I could write an entire book unpacking these eight suggestions alone. Taking the time to nurture, reflect, expand, and invest in yourself is life-changing. In my opinion, the awareness and value that come from these practices are priceless.

CREATING HEALTHY BOUNDARIES

"Givers need to set limits because takers rarely do."

—RACHEL WOLCHIN

The word boundary carries a connotative or negative association. Whether it be personal, professional, or political—why do we have such a problem with boundaries? Why do we feel guilt for building barriers to protect ourselves?

Setting boundaries in relationships is not a matter of keeping yourself separate but setting rules and guidelines to help navigate that social exchange in a healthy and productive manner. These boundaries you create aren't to limit yourself or close yourself off to others but to ensure others can enrich your life or add value without taking away from your own. It's a matter of creating personal statutes so that other people can't invade your life, pillage your energy, and leave you there to clean everything up.

"Compassionate people ask for what they need. They say no when they need to, and when they say yes, they mean it. They're compassionate because their boundaries keep them out of resentment."

—BRENÉ BROWN

Why do we create boundaries? Why is it beneficial in relationships?

Healthline (2018) identifies three main benefits of boundaries:

1. Better self-esteem
2. Conservation of emotional energy
3. More independence and agency

Abigail Brenner is a board-certified psychiatrist and fellow of the American Psychiatric Association. Practicing for more than thirty years, her work has focused on understanding and embracing transitions and life changes. In an article published by *Psychology Today*, she gives insight on how to create boundaries.

Dr. Brenner stresses the familiar idea of a "two-way street," explaining that these practices are put in place so that we have space to be ourselves and maintain personal integrity. She also asserts that those who still try to invade that space "clearly feel entitled to get whatever they ask for, whatever they think they need, because, of course, their needs are more important than yours" (Brenner, 2015).

"Daring to set boundaries is about having the courage to love ourselves even when we risk disappointing others."

—BRENÉ BROWN

But, how do you know if your boundaries are being crossed?

Dr. Brenner explains that these violations typically fall under one of these categories: verbal violations, psychological and emotional boundary violations, and physical violations. Other boundaries, such as moral, ethical, and spiritual, do exist as well.

What do these look like, though? How do we spot these breaches?

Brenner's (2015) examples include:

- **Verbal**: Not allowing you to speak or be heard, raising their voice, screaming at you, derogatory or inflammatory comments, gossiping about you
- **Psychological and Emotional**: Lying, criticizing, demeaning, judging, or manipulating you, making you feel guilty or responsible for them in any given situation,

making demands of your time and energy, shaming, embarrassing, or bullying you

- **Physical**: Invading your personal space without permission, violating your privacy, damaging or destroying your personal property, or threatening you with physical harm

It's crucial to note that these are only a few examples. There are endless ways another person can violate the boundaries you put in place. Half of the battle is spotting it early. Don't ignore the red flags as a means to give that person the benefit of the doubt. Too many times have I done this and gotten burned.

The world can be scary. Protect yourself out there, reader.

PSA: YOU CAN BE NUMBER ONE AND HAVE A SUPPORT SYSTEM

While autonomy has its benefits, so does connection. Social support and social integration can be incredibly beneficial to our psychological health. Research shows that poor social support, or lack thereof, is linked to depression and loneliness, which can alter cognitive function and increase the risk of alcohol use, cardiovascular disease, and suicide (Cherry, 2020).

In my research on the impact of social support, I came across these shocking statistics:

- In 2019, 61 percent of Americans reported feeling lonely (Cigna, 2020).
- Suicide is the second leading cause of death among people ages ten to thirty-four (Morin, 2021).

- According to the World Health Organization, approximately 280 million people worldwide experience depression (2021).

How can we combat these figures?

Can our support save the people around us?

According to the Mental Health Foundation (2021), more socially connected people with friends, family, or their community are happier, physically healthier, and live longer, experiencing fewer mental health problems than those who are less connected.

In what ways can we show our support, though?

In an article published by Verywell Mind, Kendra Cherry, an author, speaker, and educational consultant, discusses how social support contributes to our psychological health. According to Cherry (2020), social support can be given or received in the following forms:

- **Emotional Support**: Providing a listening ear or shoulder to cry on
- **Instrumental Support**: Taking care of your physical needs or lending a helping hand
- **Informational Support**: Providing guidance, advice, information, or mentoring

As Cherry explains, people in your social network take on different roles and provide varying types of support. While a professor may solely provide informational support, a friend or parent may provide all three. All of which are valuable and beneficial to our well-being. Ensure the connections you're building are valuable and provide you with at least one of these forms of support.

QUALITY OVER QUANTITY: BUILDING YOUR TRIBE

"Call it a clan, call it a network, call it a tribe, call it a family. Whatever you call it, whoever you are, you need one."

—JANE HOWARD

When we're younger, we instinctively long for a massive group of friends. I think part of this longing comes from being utterly perplexed with who we are and needing that external validation from absolute strangers. So, we conform and alter the version of self we present to our peers in hopes they like us. This phenomenon starts on the playground. In an article in *Psychology Today*, Joanna Cannon explains, "we begin to notice the differences between ourselves and other children, and we start to mirror the behavior of a dominant group in order to be accepted by them" (Cannon, 2016). But what happens when we successfully find that big group?

Is it all we hoped for?

I spent most of elementary and middle school in friendships that rarely went beyond the surface. With the exception of a few childhood friends, I consistently felt invisible in a large group, like no one genuinely knew who I was. Whether it be with a friend or with a romantic partner, the feeling of being utterly alone in the presence of other people is heartbreaking.

Eventually, I gave up and molded to everyone's narrative; the sweet, polite teacher's daughter. Going to the same school that my mother taught at was anything but boring. God forbid I misstep or fall short of the expectations of her colleagues; because that's a reflection of her capabilities as an educator, right?

(Don't be fooled, reader. Adults aren't any better; most of them are merely oversized children.)

Needless to say, I slowly learned how to be my own best friend. I kept a lot bottled in and was always on my best behavior. It wasn't until I reached high school that I had established those deeper connections, those ride-or-die friends I'd always wished for. Even then, I periodically had to remove myself from situations that turned toxic or no longer served me. It's not something anybody ever wants to do but necessary for our mental and emotional well-being.

Today, at the ripe age of twenty-three, I'm proud to say my careful consideration and introduction of boundaries paid off. The close friends I associate and surround myself with are some of the most loving, empathetic, hilarious human beings I've ever had the pleasure of knowing. I am consistently supported, encouraged, and never judged. My differences are finally celebrated.

"Friendship is born at that moment when one person says to another: 'What? You too! I thought I was the only one.'"

C.S. LEWIS

SEPARATE, BUT TOGETHER: ESTABLISHING BOUNDARIES WITH FAMILY AND FRIENDS

Giving family and friends access to your life can often feel like *giving a mouse a cookie.*

Naturally, the more you give, the more they want. Mom and grandma love hearing about school, but "won't you tell us about the boys, too?" If you have a loud, wildly invasive family like mine, I feel your internal struggle from here. My family is the most fun-loving, dysfunctional bunch out there—no, really, they could put *My Big Fat Greek Wedding* to shame—but I love them dearly. Despite their extremist nature, family is at the core of my values and priorities. Yet, what happens when it becomes too much? What happens when we need space to grow?

How do we effectively enforce boundaries with the most important people in our life? Refer back to Dr. Brenner's insights. Make sure you're able to recognize what unhealthy boundaries and breaches look like.

In an article published by *Psychology Today,* Dr. Rachel Zoffness discusses boundaries as it relates to family (2019). A great piece of advice she gives is to know your triggers and be able to anticipate them. From witnessing your parents coddle a younger sibling to "your cousin Barbara sticking her fingers in the Christmas ham," triggers can be wide-ranging. Dr. Zoffness gives four steps to rectify these situations:

1. Identify what your triggers are.
2. Recognize the emotions that arise from them.
3. Evaluate how to best cope.
4. Plan your response.

Sometimes those closest to us aren't aware of how their behavior affects us. Gently bring these things to their attention and enforce those healthy boundaries!

SUCK OUT THE VENOM: ELIMINATING TOXICITY AND HALF-ASS RELATIONSHIPS

"They say nothing lasts forever; dreams change, trends come and go, but friendships never go out of style."

—CARRIE BRADSHAW, *SEX AND THE CITY*

Disclaimer: Please do not try this if actually bitten by a snake. It is indeed a myth.

However, it makes a fantastic analogy to discuss unhealthy relationships.

From time to time, we find ourselves wandering through the garden of life. Metamorphic butterflies, fickle frogs, and even a snake is bound to cross our path. When we come face-to-face with this slimy creature, we're unsure how to proceed at first. So, we stand frozen, waiting for its next move. This secretive serpent senses our fear and nervousness but asserts its dominance. There are no sudden movements, so we carry on our way. Yet, just as the wind hits our back, a pair of razor-sharp teeth dig into our Achilles heel, bringing us to our knees.

My father always told me that friends inevitably fall into one of two categories: family or acquaintance. He used to say, "you find out real quick who's going to have your back when the shit hits the fan." Those individuals become chosen family, and the rest fall by the wayside. There doesn't have to be animosity or bad blood, but some people are just not meant for you. Hell, some people genuinely can't handle supporting and celebrating you. Envy is a green-eyed monster that slowly eats away at one's relationships. It's a shape-shifter, really; trying on different forms, tones, and characters until you're standing there alone, blaming everyone around you.

Love, health, wellness, and boundaries begin with you, reader. No matter what relationship in your life, you decide what you accept. You want to accept toxicity and poison into your bloodstream? Go for it. If you want to cling onto half-ass people who give no effort or provide minimal value to your life, be my guest. *But* it's all in your hands. In this predicament, you and only you decide your fate.

"I will not let anyone walk through my mind with their dirty feet."

—MAHATMA GANDHI

THE ROAD TO EMOTIONAL FULFILLMENT: HEALTH WITHIN LOVE AND DATING

"Just because we're deserving of love does not mean we are excused from the work that's required for a relationship to thrive. Relationships don't thrive because we rest in our innate worthiness. Relationships thrive because the participants dive in, have hard conversations, face parts of themselves they've historically denied, and hold up mirrors for one another over and over again."

—VIENNA PHARAON

I used to believe love was simply a feeling; a warm feeling in the pit of your stomach, a sense of home, a feeling of comfort and safety, unspoken chemistry and connection between individuals, a sacred bond, and acceptance of someone in their entirety. Yet, it is not. Love isn't simply a feeling or a noun. Love is a verb, a choice followed by action, and not an easy one at that. Someone can have love for you but still not choose to love you. This is where things become tricky and confusing. Love is a word used by many but truly understood by few.

Why is there such a lack of understanding within love and romantic relationships, though?

Two years ago, I pondered this exact topic in a journal entry.

December 5th, 2019:

Let's talk about love for a few minutes here. You know that four-letter word everyone is scared of but secretly dying to have and holds the weight of a 74,000 lb. dump truck? We place so much pressure and silly expectations on this word that by the time we are holding it in our hands, we might not even recognize it. Or, better yet, we could easily mess it all up. Can we, as a collective whole, decide to redefine and refine the way we view love? Can we throw away these superficial, unrealistic, one-size-fits-all norms? Can we throw out the rule book?

Love is a lot of things, but perfect is definitely not one of them. I don't know what clown made up this word, but the word "perfection" really puts a monkey-wrench in many aspects of life, does it not? This word alone creates expectations that are not realistic. Love may exceed your wildest dreams, but it cannot and will not ever be "perfect." Every love has flaws and downfalls. Love does not just touch the surface. It goes beneath the surface and examines your soul at a level you weren't aware was possible. Love is like two souls under a magnifying glass, exploring each other's depths. You cannot define love by age, gender, sex, or race. Love defies all these things. However, we, as humans, are the outlier. We get in the way of the natural connection and magic by sticking our two cents in and making judgments too early. Forget what society wants you to be, to look like, to act like… be you! See who finds it absolutely breathtaking and intriguing. When you're 100 percent genuinely you, see who you connect with and why.

I've never truly believed in fairytales. They were too unrealistic for me. They always made my heart warm and happy but left me questioning the validity of such circumstances. I may be a hopeless romantic and dreamer at heart, but I am realistic enough not to expect such impossibly pleasant outcomes. Yet, by exposing the youth and public to these stories and the expectations that come with them, social and gender norms are born. The media teaches little girls everywhere to think that a prince will someday sweep them off their feet and take care of them. Then in return, teaches little boys to feel that they must always be strong, heroic, and do the saving. How is this fair or realistic in any manner? This narrative has progressed some over the years, but most forms of storytelling still fail to fully depict the trials and tribulations of love. The princess doesn't just land the prince and live happily ever after. There is, in fact, more to the story.

Rarely do we see stories about the harsh realities of married life...why is this? Is it because it might ruin the magic and mystery? Excuse me if I think that's bullshit. That theory ends up creating impracticable expectations and ultimately contributing to the giant miscommunication between men and women, as well as the misunderstanding surrounding love and romantic relationships. Does anyone consider this? I believe there is still magic, mystery, wonder, and happiness to be found in marriage, childbirth, raising children, and empty-nesting. It's not the beginning of a story that moves people. It's the journey. It's acknowledging the beginning, seeing the struggles, the ups, the downs, the love, the endless trials, and how those two people choose each other despite the hardship they may face. And hell, maybe they don't choose each other! Perhaps they end up choosing themselves and deciding they aren't supposed to build a life together. Either way, it is the journey that is more beautiful, realistic, and bittersweet. The media should portray this more. To creators, authors, and storytellers everywhere, tell the whole goddamn story or don't tell it at all. Love, yours truly.

The truth is, love requires work. It also requires patience, strength, and compromise. Each day, choices present themselves that inevitably dictate how we prioritize and manage our time. Love is something we must choose to put our time, efforts, and energy toward, whether it is love for ourselves, for others around us, or even for the world and communities in which we inhabit.

I've spent far too long complicating and pondering the idea of love and all that surrounds it. When truthfully, it boils down to mindset, just like everything else in life. You can choose to make situations incomprehensibly impossible, or you can decide to go after what you want and make your dreams a reality. It *can* be that simple.

THROUGH THE LOOKING GLASS: WHAT IS "HEALTHY" LOVE?

"A healthy relationship is one in which love enriches you; not imprisons you."

—STEVE MARABOLI

As messy and confusing as love and dating become, there's always something new to learn. Even while exploring or getting to know someone else, you end up seeing new sides of yourself. As we examine another soul, we concurrently peel back deeper layers of our own. Not everyone will be the right person for you, but they will always provide you with a lesson to carry with you for the person who is.

I don't believe there is such thing as "your other half," "better half," or "the one." We are complete on our own; a partner is simply an addition that can complement your worthiness. Therefore, protecting your energy and your needs is essential. I don't mean this in the sense of putting up walls and creating roadblocks to your heart. I'm talking about continuing to live and breathe *for you*. Your wants, needs, and desires before you enter a relationship still matter and need to be accounted for afterward. You cannot completely lose sight of who you are as an individual, even if you enter a relationship.

We can't ever know if someone is "forever," to mine and any overthinker's dismay, so why hold each potential suitor up to this fictional character you've never met but carefully curated in your head. Instead, take people as they are and continuously evaluate if and how that person serves you or enriches your life. This is really all we can do.

BULLSHIT FREE: RECIPE FOR A HEALTHY RELATIONSHIP

Out of human nature, we gravitate toward love. We crave connection and companionship. So why, after all this time, are we so bad at it? *How can we be better not only for ourselves but for our partners?*

After research, extensive contemplation, and some experience of my own, I have formulated a list of ingredients to nourish and ensure the connection you're creating is healthy.

Trust and Transparency

Michael J. Formica is a board-certified counselor, integral life coach, teacher, and self-development expert. In an article published by *Psychology Today,* he emphasizes the importance of transparency and how it allows partners to feel safe or develop a sense of security and consistency in their relationship (Formica, 2010). Practicing transparency diminishes potential conflict, fear, anxiety, and overthinking. Something as simple as texting your partner "On my way" can make more of a difference than you think. Open and honest communication allows partners to feel more comfortable expressing their wants, needs, fears, desires, and innermost thoughts. When two people are able and willing to communicate on such a transparent level, they can better fulfill each other's relational needs.

Transparency fosters trust. *Trust* is the glue that holds this union together. When partners can communicate openly and honestly, it not only increases the trust in their relationship but strengthens the bond they share.

Communication

Formica claims, "We are the only species on the planet that has been gifted with symbolic language, yet we often fail to use it in its most effective capacity" (2010).

Communication supports this idea of transparency. Consistently put your thoughts, ideas, and feelings on the table. Let your partner know where your head is at, rather than walking on eggshells or beating around the bush. Confront conflict with resolution. Express your concerns and find a way to come to a joint solution. Allow space for discomfort, for, without it, we cannot grow.

Avoiding confrontation and dismissing problems within a relationship is a *red flag*. You should be having hard conversations and engaging in healthy confrontation once in a while. When conflict does arise, remember this—It's not you versus your partner. Take off the gloves, Rocky! It's the two of you versus the problem.

Compromise and Understanding

Everyone wants to feel heard, accepted, and understood. When your partner speaks, listen. In return, make sure you have a partner capable of listening to your wants and needs. Healthy relationships require compromise, where both parties' needs, wants, and desires are being heard and met. This requires a tremendous amount of patience and consideration from both parties. Both of you can't always get everything you desire. Sometimes one will have to bend for the other, and vice versa. Love isn't easy, and both parties must be willing to put in the work to help this union flourish. The reality is it can't be 50/50 all the time.

Respect
The key to establishing boundaries and healthy relationships, whether romantic or platonic, is mutual respect. Formica explains that actions like chronically being late or saying one thing then doing another all portray a lack of respect and consideration (2010). Having knowledge and the utmost consideration for the things that are most important to each partner is key.

Shared Responsibility
What does shared responsibility look like in a relationship? It comes mainly in the form of shared time and effort. From complacent married couples to teenage puppy love, responsibility matters. Whether it be household duties or planning picture-perfect dates, all of the weight shouldn't fall on one party's shoulders. Instead, take turns. Find a split that works for you both and keep each other accountable.

Reciprocity
Reciprocity is the simple idea of mutual action and reaction. In relationships, we see this in the form of affection, intimacy, attention, patience, warmth, kindness, etc. Making an effort to meet your partner, or rather reciprocate their actions, is important. One person can't carry the relationship. Reciprocity is work. I believe reciprocity is what keeps the love alive in a marriage. A mutual exchange of effort and

adoration can make thirty years of marriage still feel like dating. Take the time for the little things; getting your partner flowers, asking them about their day, or simply texting them good morning. Make time for date night. Make time for intimacy. What you put into this union is exactly what you will get out of it.

Much like communication and transparency, intimacy and affection help strengthen that bond, further strengthening the trust within a union. Everyone desires to be wanted and chosen. Make sure you're taking the time to understand *how* to love your partner. What is their love language, and how can you successfully fulfill it? Take notes and do your research, ladies and gentlemen.

"Abundance is a dance with reciprocity—what we can give, what we can share, and what we receive in the process."

—TERRY TEMPEST WILLIAMS

HUMAN CONNECTION: A COLLECTION OF EPIC NOVELS, SHORT STORIES, AND IMPROPER FRAGMENTS

"Colors fade, temples crumble, empires fall, but wise words endure."

—EDWARD THORNDIKE

Whether it be family, friends, or romantic partners, we're constantly searching for a story. We wander aimlessly through life, searching for supporting roles in the tangled web we weave. Some stay for a while. Others come and go in the blink of an eye, disrupting our life like a tornado.

Carrie Bradshaw once said, "some love stories aren't epic novels—some are short stories, but that doesn't make them any less filled with love." This is true of all relationships in one's lifetime. People will come and go like the seasons, but *you* are the constant.

Not everyone in your life is meant to stay. Some will come in and teach you lessons you would have never learned otherwise. Some will challenge, test, and bulldoze over old versions of you to make way for new ones. Others will stand the test of time and be complementary to your growth. You may meet people that end up staying a lifetime, supporting, loving, and prioritizing your presence in their life. All of which is par for the course.

The greatest advice I can give you is to *choose wisely*. Not everyone will have a supporting role. Some are simply supposed to watch from the sidelines.

CHAPTER 6

OUR SCARS
HOLD STORIES

"My scars tell a story. They are a reminder of times when life tried to break me but failed. They are markings of where the structure of my character was welded."

—STEVE MARABOLI

Just like the sharp edge of a knife, our experiences cut deep into our supple flesh leaving behind open wounds and damaged tissue. Tissues of which take time and immense care to heal, and even when they've healed, our skin is never the same. Scars remain, reminding us of the experiences that pierce below the surface. Warmer hues of purple and blush remind us of our origins. They remind us at the end of the day, we're only human. We're neither invincible nor indestructible. We may be warriors taking on each day with tougher skin, yet we still remain vulnerable, fragile, and malleable. Each scar holds a story. Each ridge and puckered edge is a constant reminder of the battles we've endured.

"One day, you will tell your story of how you overcame what you went through, and it will be someone else's survival guide."

—BRENÉ BROWN

In this life, one single moment can change the course of your entire existence. One day can be crippling. One word can make us come apart at the seams. However, *one choice* can reverse all of that. The choice to pick yourself up, dust yourself off, and carry on is the most important choice you can make every day.

I believe the hardest part about embracing your individual journey is accepting both the good and the bad. It's about accepting all the horrible things you've endured and choosing to view them in a different light. These experiences changed you, whether for the better or the worst, and it's up to you to choose how you let these experiences affect you. Perspective and attitude are a choice. Take that trauma and turn it into a lesson. Move forward, knowing you are stronger because of everything you've been through. Your trauma doesn't define you, nor does it make you broken, weak, or damaged. You are only broken if you choose to stay that way.

You have all the strength you need to pick yourself up, piece yourself back together, and be whoever you want to be. Your stories, your trauma, and your scars might just be someone else's guide to survival. The lessons learned within those scars hold the power to save someone else.

"You never know how strong you are until being strong is your only choice."

—BOB MARLEY

I once felt broken and alone. In the midst of my life falling apart, I felt like an army of one. Even though I had a support system of people desperately trying to help me, they were just as lost and didn't grasp the full extent of what I was going through.

Ponder this for a moment:

Can another person genuinely comprehend or feel the wars waging inside of you?

Can they see what's eating you alive? Or are they somewhat blind to it?

In my experience, most people cannot.

The love and support from family and friends was so appreciated, but truthfully, they didn't know how to help me. And for a while, I didn't know how to help myself either.

It's like learning how to walk again. You have to crawl through the wreckage before you can start to take steps to clean everything up. I had entered uncharted territory with no survival guide. I had to recognize what I'd lost, grieve, and mourn the life I once knew or was familiar with, so I could move forward. I had to research and become familiar with this new way of living and being. I had to fight for answers.

I had to pick myself up off the ground and advocate for my needs. I had to change my frame of thinking and choose to look at the blessings in my life on a daily basis. I had to recognize everything I'd gained in my destruction. My life may have caught fire, but I had to learn how to dance in the flames.

"In her heart and soul, she set fire to all things that held her back, and from the ashes, she stepped into who she always was."

—ATTICUS

THOSE WHO WALKED BEFORE US: PERSEVERING THROUGH GREAT ODDS

More often than not, our triumphs are publicized rather than our failures, pain, or the traumatic experiences we go through. Few people actually see or know what goes on behind closed doors. Rarely do we advertise or post about the things that haunt us or leave a permanent mark on our journey. A great number of people fail to recognize even the very best of us have baggage. Some of the most accomplished individuals in history experienced trauma of some kind and came out stronger in spite of it.

"You never know what someone is dealing with behind closed doors. You only know what you see or what you think you see."

—MACKENZIE PHILLIPS

I have loved old, classic films for as long as I can remember. Given that, it should come as no shock my favorite actress is, without a doubt, Audrey Hepburn. Since her debut in *Roman Holiday* (1953), the silver screen has yet to see another with her caliber of talent, vulnerability, and childlike wonder. Although most of society knows Audrey for her timeless style, class, and humanitarian heart, she endured great hardship early on that left a lasting impact on her life.

Audrey was born on May 4th, 1929, in Belgium. She was only five years old when her mother packed her things and sent her to a boarding school in England (Biography, 2020). While she was away, tensions grew, and it wasn't long before her parents divorced. Her father leaving and abandoning her family proved to be one of the most "defining moments of her life" (Biography, 2020). By 1940, Nazi Germany had invaded Holland, where she and her family were currently residing. Audrey faced German occupation, world war, famine, and extensive malnutrition. Everyone admires and praises Audrey for her slim figure, but rarely do we take into account that it's due to the prolonged trauma she faced. Audrey later experienced multiple miscarriages due to her health.

While her early life may have been torturous, her legacy and talent live on. Later in her life, Audrey dedicated her efforts to humanitarian work with UNICEF. By 1989, she dedicated herself to United Nations relief efforts for children. Deeply touched by the role UNICEF played in her own life, she felt she had an obligation and purpose to give back (Biography, 2020).

"I believe in being strong when everything seems to be going wrong. I believe that happy girls are the prettiest girls. I believe that tomorrow is another day, and I believe in miracles."

—AUDREY HEPBURN

Oprah Gail Winfrey is an American talk show host, television producer, actress, author, and philanthropist. She was inducted into the National Women's Hall of Fame in 1994 as the first African American woman to own her own production company. She is one of television's highest-paid entertainers, reaching nearly fifteen million people daily. While most Americans are familiar with Oprah and her many achievements, most are unaware of her traumatic upbringing.

Born January 29, 1954, Oprah grew up in rural Mississippi. Her parents were poverty-stricken teenagers, and their relationship didn't last long. They sent her to live with her grandmother for the first six years of her life. As she got older, she moved to Wisconsin with her mother. During her time at both homes, she was repeatedly beaten, molested by male relatives, and exposed to toxic situations. (Doctor Oz, 2021). After later moving to Nashville with her father, she began her career in broadcasting. Although her career excelled and she became a public figure, she continued to face scrutiny. Whether it be her weight, her sex, or her race, she battled against the people and things that tried to hold her back. She's spent decades connecting with others, sharing their stories, and sharing her "post-traumatic wisdom" (Doctor Oz, 2021).

"Challenges are gifts that force us to search for a new center of gravity. Don't fight them. Just find a new way to stand."

—OPRAH WINFREY

Both of these divine female trailblazers actually share an impressive achievement. Both Audrey Hepburn and Oprah Winfrey have received the United States' highest civilian award, the Presidential Medal of Freedom. Hepburn received the award in 1992, and Winfrey received it in 2013. The Presidential Medal of Freedom established by President John F. Kennedy in 1963 is given to individuals who "make an especially meritorious contribution to the security or national interests of the United States, world peace, cultural or other significant public or private endeavors." These two, as well as other decorated recipients, go to show that no adversity, hardship, or obstacle is too large to overcome. Additionally, trauma does not define the individual. Neither of these stars are known for their struggles. They are known for their triumphs. We see their legacy in how they showed service and in the ways they chose to give back to their communities.

MY JOURNEY TO NOW

To tell one's story or unpack one's trauma is no easy task. I certainly have not gone through what the icons described above have, yet that doesn't invalidate my journey or make my experiences any less significant.

Throughout the process of writing this book, I've relived and reexperienced a lot of that trauma, leaving me to question if any of it was ever truly resolved or whether the idea of sharing it with you was just terrifying...most likely a combination of both.

I've spent months on end revisiting past wounds and tracing old scars in search of meaning and valuable lessons to share with you, reader. Much like what I went through years prior, I realized my past trauma and insecurities spanned much farther than my health. It just took getting to that breaking point to unpack the rest of it.

Living with an undiagnosed autoimmune disease in an environment that wasn't conducive for me led me down a desolate rabbit hole. As dark and twisty as that was, the inevitable depression that came along with my conditions at the time allowed me to finally process the pain and grief I'd suppressed all my life. I'd finally allowed myself to actually *feel* *it*. I'd finally allowed myself to feel everything and everyone that had broken a piece of me; broken parts that I'd spent so much time hiding and concealing from everyone around me. I allowed myself to fully examine all I'd endured until I made sense of it, until I felt that weight finally lifted from my chest. I may have let that darkness swallow me whole, but I eventually fought my way back to the surface, coming up for air.

As healing as this writing process has been, it's been incredibly difficult to revisit my trauma and that time of my life. Some days have been mentally and emotionally crippling. Others have been so enlightening and filled with gratitude.

"My home betrayed me."

—ANONYMOUS

I came across a social media post from a mutual friend of mine, and these words have stuck with me since. For years, I've been trying to piece together how my disease has changed my life. Truthfully, it's changed me for the better. It's forced me to put myself and my health first. It's forced me to challenge myself and face my fears. It's forced me to live without limitations and to love even the most undesirable parts of myself. Yet, for the longest time, I think I held on to this fear, shame, and guilt because my body failed me. I've held onto shame and guilt because my body *"isn't like everybody else's."*

My "home" quite literally betrayed me and attacked itself from within.

I wasn't diagnosed with my autoimmune disease until 2017. I had been experiencing symptoms and abnormalities linked to Hashimoto's for over three years prior. So, when doctors finally ran the proper blood panel, I was an absolute train wreck by the time of my diagnosis. My body was weak, unstable, and heavy to bear. On the outside, I may have appeared optimistic and strong, but on the inside, I was barely functioning.

If I'm being completely transparent, the hardest part about my experience wasn't the physical pain and distress. It was the mental and emotional battles that came along with it. It was the everyday struggles that occurred beneath the surface that weren't visible to any outsider. It was the feeling of being supported yet feeling utterly alone in my fight. It was the feeling of being constantly in conflict or at war with the very vessel that serves me. It was the feeling of constantly trying to dig myself out of a hole I didn't intentionally put myself in.

"You need to spend time crawling alone through shadows to truly appreciate what it is to stand in the sun."

—SHAUN HICK

I hadn't admitted to myself until recently that for a long time after my diagnosis, I lived in fear; fear that my body would betray me again. I feared even if I did everything "right," or everything medical professionals instructed me to do, my body would self-destruct again. I was living every day in survival mode, a way of being that is, unfortunately, familiar to me. Even today, it is a daily tug of war with myself not to naturally go into that mindset. My experiences with my health and my autoimmune disease have caused me to distrust my body. In the past, I have failed to accept and acknowledge the pain, high functioning anxiety, and fear this health journey has added to my life. This book has forced me to look those demons in the face each day and choose to silence them before they have the chance to eat me alive. You deserve to hear my story, as frightening as it may be for me to tell.

I may never see combat, but my body has experienced war.

THE WAR WITHIN: WHAT IS TRAUMA AND HOW IS IT AFFECTING YOUR LIFE?

"There are wounds that never show on the body that are deeper and more hurtful than anything that bleeds.

—LAURELL K. HAMILTON

Although this life is transformative and beautiful, it can also be very scary. Whether you reside in a bubble or take the world head-on every day, we all face challenges at one point or another. Our experiences can make or break us. Many of us have some form of trauma, stress, or anxiety as a direct result of these experiences. One traumatic event can be debilitating. Prolonged trauma can be not only mentally and emotionally taxing but damaging to your physical health.

Allow me to take a moment and share some shocking statistics about trauma with you:

- Seventy percent of adults in the US have experienced some type of traumatic event at least once in their lives. That's 223.4 million people. (The National Council for Behavioral Health, 2020).
- In the United States, a woman is beaten every fifteen seconds, and a forcible rape occurs every six minutes. (The National Council for Behavioral Health, 2020).
- Of people in the United States who experience a traumatic event, up to 20 percent of these individuals will go on to develop post-traumatic stress disorder or PTSD. (Sidran Institute, 2018)
- Women are about twice as likely as men to develop PTSD. (Sidran Institute, 2018)
- More than 33 percent of youth exposed to community violence will experience PTSD, a very severe reaction to traumatic events. (The National Council for Behavioral Health, 2020).

As you can see, trauma isn't actually so uncommon. It's just not discussed nearly enough as it should be. Why is that, though? Sure, all of our trauma looks and feels different, but would it not be beneficial to talk about it anyway? Wouldn't this only help to increase understanding and empathy?

What exactly is *trauma,* though?

According to the American Psychological Association (APA), trauma is "an emotional response to a terrible event like an accident, rape, or natural disaster" (2020). However, I believe trauma is much more than this definition. Trauma is messy, complicated, and expansive. Trauma can cause a range of different responses (physically, mentally, and emotionally) and can present in so many forms. Just as humans come in all shapes and sizes, our trauma is no different. There is no one-size-fits-all model to assess, treat, or cope with trauma.

THE SLEEPING GIANT: UNRESOLVED TRAUMA

"Unresolved emotional pain is the great contagion of our time— of all-time."

—MARC IAN BARASCH

Unpacking trauma can either feel like an episode of hoarders or attempting to find a needle in a haystack of experiences. Nonetheless, it's important to know what you're looking for. What are the different types of unresolved trauma, and how can we effectively identify them within our own personal landscape?

Types of Unresolved Trauma (Psych2Go, 2020):

Big T Trauma:
This type of unresolved trauma comes from single traumatic events that can leave lasting impacts on an individual. Symptoms typically include nightmares, flashbacks, and intrusive or negative thoughts. Big T trauma can often result from

sexual assault, acts of terrorism, war, prolonged physical, emotional, or sexual abuse.

Small T Trauma:

Small T Trauma can often trace back to traumatic events that result from personal events. Examples might include job termination, divorce, continuous academic, financial, and personal stress, etc.

Acute Trauma:

Acute trauma occurs from a single event (which can fall under Big T or Small T). Examples may include witnessing an act of violence, assault, house fire, or car accident.

Chronic Trauma:

Chronic trauma is a form of repeated or prolonged trauma. This is most commonly a result of domestic violence, ongoing abuse, medical trauma, bullying, or war.

Complex Trauma:

Just like the name, this type of unresolved trauma associates with people who experience multiple forms of trauma throughout their lifetime. Those who grow up in a chaotic home environment and then go on to face other traumatic events in life are a perfect example.

Trauma is incredibly complex, hence why I'm a huge supporter of therapy. Talking aloud to someone completely disconnected from your network about suppressed memories can be life-changing. Sometimes we need someone who's not inside our head or in any way involved to give us a dose of reality and insight.

Some of the most common forms of unresolved trauma stem from childhood. This can come in the form of abuse, neglect, mental health issues, serious injury, serious illness, problems at school, etc. An estimated 15 percent to 43 percent of children experience at least one trauma during their childhood (Dobric, 2021). Research, time and time again, has proven that such experiences affect brain development. Moments may be brief, but they can have lifelong impacts. Traumatic experiences have the power to evolve into mental health problems, social thinning, or latent vulnerability.

"The greater a child's terror, and the earlier it is experienced, the harder it becomes to develop a strong and healthy sense of self."

—NATHANIEL BRANDEN

Reminder: You are more than what's happened to you. Trauma doesn't have to ruin your life. You have a choice in how trauma affects your life.

EXPERIENCE: THE CONNECTIVE TISSUE

"Experience is the connective tissue between the questions we have and the answers we seek."

—UNKNOWN

These examples and different forms of unresolved trauma have the power and ability to lead to PTSD, "which affects about 8 percent of Americans at some time in their lives." (Bremner, 2006).

So, how does this progression happen?

How do the traumatic events we experience, or even unresolved forms of trauma, affect us?

Oh, What A Tangled Web We Weave: How Does Trauma Effect Your Brain?

Most research conducted to investigate trauma's effect on the human brain is done on combat veterans. Within these research studies, there are some common findings. According to the American Museum of Natural History (2012), studies indicate that traumatic experiences during war or combat have the ability to shrink a brain region known as the hippocampus. For any who are not familiar, the hippocampus is primarily responsible for memory and learning, as well as regulating emotional responses (Britannica, 2021). This region, located in the frontal lobe, "plays a crucial role in the formation, organization, and storage of new memories as well as connecting certain sensations and emotions to these memories (Kendra Cherry, 2020). Given, serious injury to this vital instrument can lead to various detrimental short-term and long-term effects. Not only does trauma have the ability to shrink your hippocampus over time, but in a traumatic event, the sudden release of the stress hormone, cortisol, can directly kill brain cells within this region (American Museum of Natural History, 2012).

Lethal to the Human Body: Let's Talk Cortisol

"Trauma produces actual physiological changes, including a recalibration of the brain's alarm system, an increase in stress hormone."

—BESSEL A. VAN DER KOLK, THE BODY KEEPS THE SCORE: BRAIN, MIND, AND BODY IN THE HEALING OF TRAUMA

According to the National Institute of Stress (2020), the fight-or-flight response, also referred to as the acute stress response, refers to a physiological reaction that occurs in the presence of a threat. We're humans with an "animal instinct." When something frightens us, this response triggers the release of hormones in our body, preparing us to either fight the threat or run to safety. We experience an increase in adrenaline, elevated blood pressure, and the release of the stress hormone cortisol (Mayo Clinic, 2021). Once a perceived threat has passed, our hormone levels return to normal. However, when stress is consistently prevalent in our life, our body continues to feel like it's under attack. Therefore, it continues to produce cortisol.

Long-term activation of this stress hormone wreaks havoc on the human body, putting us at risk for anxiety, depression, chronic disease, digestive issues, headaches, weight gain, insomnia, memory impairment, and so on (Mayo Clinic, 2021).

We live in a world that is always moving and naturally stressful. How can we lower cortisol and decrease stress on the mind and body?

We can go back to the basics!

Circling back to Maslow's lower-level needs is essential. Making sure you're eating a nutritious diet, sleeping enough, and finding ways to de-stress is crucial. Whether it be yoga, strength training, or breathing exercises—find what works for you. It's likely one of those needs isn't being met or managed properly. Evaluate your environment, your behaviors, and the stressful triggers within them.

TRAINED TO BE "STRONG"

Even as children, we are taught to be strong or to put on a brave face. Society trains us to hide our fear, our pain, and our deepest feelings from our neighbors. Just like soldiers, we place ourselves in camouflage and walk through the chaos, expected to be unfazed. The expectation is for us to be unchanged as we walk down a road that's constantly changing right beneath our feet. So, what happens when we come home at the end of the day, and our mask comes off? Can we still keep it together? How do we deal with those emotions and experiences?

How do we cope?

When you were a child, did you experience the ever-so-common irrational fear of thinking there was a monster underneath your bed?

If you did, what effect did this fear have on you? Did it make you want to run and hide? Maybe even avoid your room all together?

This is an experience many people can relate to. During our youth, we are not only more aware of our fears but more expressive about them. We are more open to sharing them with others, not ashamed by what others may think of us. As children develop into adults, they no longer fear the monster under the bed but rather the one in their head, the one expressing their fears and insecurities to them. They no longer express these fears out loud, fearing that these words may hold truth. We then fear others will judge us for these truths.

They never tell you as a kid that the monsters to hide from are projected fears, self-doubt, and insecurity.

—SONYA TECLAI

When we experience a traumatic event, we most commonly experience the following reactions:

Avoidance

Avoidance is "any action designed to prevent the occurrence of an uncomfortable emotion such as fear, sadness, or shame" (Tull, 2020). Dissociation and substance abuse are examples of this.

While emotional avoidance may be effective in the short-term and provide temporary relief, in the long run, it can cause increased severity of PTSD symptoms (Tull, 2020). Bottling up those emotions and experiences may sound good at the moment, but they're guaranteed to resurface.

Dissociation

Dissociation, a form of avoidance, can be defined as "a disconnection between a person's thoughts, memories, feelings, actions or sense of who he or she is" (American Psychiatric Association, 2018). Mild, or more "mainstream," examples of this include daydreaming, highway hypnosis, or "getting lost" in a book or movie, all of which involve "losing touch" with awareness of one's immediate surroundings. In terms of coping with trauma, people may choose to distract or "dissociate" themselves to deal with thoughts and feelings that are too difficult to bear. Rather than facing our trauma, sometimes it's easier to distract ourselves and simply pretend it's not there. We see extremely mild cases of this even in people who have never experienced trauma but experience stress in their daily life.

In more extreme cases, dissociative behaviors can lead to various mental or dissociative disorders such as depersonalization-derealization disorder, dissociative identity disorder, dissociative amnesia, borderline personality disorder (BPD), obsessive-compulsive disorder (OCD), PTSD, Schizophrenia, and more. Our brain is fragile. We must be mindful of how we're using it.

Emotional Numbing

Emotional numbing is another coping mechanism within avoidance cluster behaviors. When we are emotionally numb, we may experience symptoms like feeling distant from others, losing interest in activities, or having difficulty experiencing positive feelings like joy or love (Tull, 2020).

"We deny, suppress, repress, and minimize our trauma to preserve our self-concept. By doing so, we set ourselves up for repeating the cycle again."

—KENNY WEISS, *YOUR JOURNEY TO SUCCESS: HOW TO ACCEPT THE ANSWERS YOU DISCOVER ALONG THE WAY*

DEBUNKING THE STIGMA

"Feeling out of control, survivors of trauma often begin to fear that they are damaged to the core and beyond redemption."

— BESSEL A. VAN DER KOLK, *THE BODY KEEPS THE SCORE: BRAIN, MIND, AND BODY IN THE HEALING OF TRAUMA*

There is a vast misconception about trauma. We see an example of this, especially within dating and relationships. There's this unrealistic, societal belief we all adopt at one point or another; that there's someone, somewhere out there for us, who is "normal" or doesn't have "baggage."

If you can feel my eyeballs rolling into the back of their sockets from here... you'd be correct. There is so much wrong with this. Once again, WTF is "normal"? Second, *all* of us have baggage. Our baggage just comes in different shapes and sizes, just like everything else. Not only that but isn't normal in the eye of the beholder? Who's to say what's big and what's small?

Now ask yourself: How is trauma any different?

People stiffen just hearing the word trauma. The word itself has such a connotation or negative association that it often prevents individuals from seeking help. The stigma that surrounds trauma is enough to discourage someone from getting the proper treatment.

Why are we so ashamed to seek help?

While this trend is more common among combat veterans, it is not limited to the average individual. Some of us live among our trauma for so long that we can no longer recognize common symptoms, signs, reactions, or triggered responses. People would rather bury their trauma than associate or label themselves with problems, trauma, or even PTSD, in fear that others may label them as "damaged."

On average, about 30 percent of first responders are diagnosed with PTSD and depression, and the number of suicides among veterans is 17.6 per day (Dobric, 2021).

Our experiences shape our behaviors. They are the connective tissue that shapes who we become. We need to start discussing these traumatic experiences rather than fearing judgment from those around us. We can help each other through the storm.

LEARNING HOW TO COPE AND GROW FROM YOUR EXPERIENCES

Sometimes we feel like we're in the eye of a storm, surrounded by walls of high-speed confusion and debris. It's hard to see beyond the wreckage, let alone find your way out. When it all feels too overwhelming, how can we cope in a healthy manner?

The National Council for Behavioral Health (2020) recommends the following coping strategies:

1. Acknowledge Your Trauma
2. Connect with Others
3. Exercise
4. Relax
5. Dive into Music, Art, etc.
6. Maintain a Balanced Diet and Sleep Cycle
7. Avoid Excess Consumption of Stimulants
8. Commit to Meaning
9. Write

In addition to social support and self-monitoring, Cognitive Behavioral Therapy (CBT) and Acceptance and Commitment Therapy (ACT) may be incredibly helpful (Tull, 2020). Not everyone believes in therapy, which I respect, but I'm a huge advocate. It can be life-changing if you whole-heartedly give it a try. Sometimes having someone who's completely unrelated to your problems is exactly what you need to navigate your way through them.

HOW TO BE A SUPPORTER

Maybe you're not the one with trauma or stressful experiences. Maybe it's your partner, your friend, or your family member. So, how do you help this person? What is your role in their journey?

In an article published by HuffPost, Nicole Pajer presents thirteen small ways in which you can support someone who has experienced trauma. Here are a few I found most helpful:

1. Realize that trauma can resurface.
2. Know that little gestures go a long way.
3. Be patient, give space, and don't force them to talk about it.
4. Educate yourself.
5. Suggest a support group.

Trauma isn't one-size-fits-all, and neither is supporting it. Remember, you're there for support and comfort, not to "fix" them.

Additional Resources for Support:

- Substance Abuse and Mental Health Services Administration (SAMHSA) National Helpline at (1-800-662-4357)
- National Suicide Prevention Lifeline (1-800-273-8255)
- Crisis Text Line (Text CONNECT to 741741)

CONFRONTING CONFLICT AND SEEING BEYOND YOUR OWN TRAUMA

"There is wisdom in the diversity of our wounds."

—MASTIN KIPP

Mastin Kipp is a best-selling author, speaker, and Creator of Functional Life Coaching. In 2019, he gave a TEDx Talk about systematic, unhealed, and unresolved trauma. He discusses chronic social trauma experiences we may encounter as a society like racism, classism, economic inequality, sexism, ageism, misogyny, xenophobia, political polarization, and mass incarceration (2019). Kipp explains that "in order to change a thing, you have to understand a thing," and emotional trauma is simply an explanation, not an excuse for behavior.

How do we heal, though? How do we confront conflict and see beyond our messy, collective trauma?

He presents the three phases of healing emotional trauma: denying, acknowledging, and transcending. He also presents a concept called the "transitional character" (TEDx, 2019).

"A transitional character is one who, in a single generation, changes the entire course of a lineage. Who somehow find a way to metabolize the poison and refuse to pass it on to their children. They break the mold. Their contribution to humanity is to filter the destructiveness out of their own lineage so that the generations downstream will have a supportive foundation upon which to build productive lives."

—DR. CARLFRED BRODERICK, PHD

Becoming a transitional character is about validating, empathizing, connecting, repairing, and setting new limits, and it starts with *you*.

LIGHT AT THE END OF THE TUNNEL: EVEN IN TRAGEDY, THERE IS MAGIC

"I have come to the conclusion that human beings are born with an innate capacity to triumph over trauma. I believe not only that trauma is curable, but that the healing process can be a catalyst for profound awakening—a portal opening to emotional and genuine spiritual transformation."

—PETER A. LEVINE, HEALING TRAUMA: A PIONEERING PROGRAM FOR RESTORING THE WISDOM OF YOUR BODY

Each day in this life is not only a gift but a test. A test of how well we handle the curveballs the universe throws at us. At the end of a bad day, are you still able to see the love, the light, and the magic?

Can you hold onto hope and faith that things will turn around?

Are you able to realize how much you're loved and how fortunate you are just to be breathing?

Trauma and pain are a result of the messy, confusing journey we're on in life, but they don't have to define who we are as individuals. Our scars do, in fact, hold stories. Stories that are at times tragic, difficult, and excruciating to talk about, but stories that have shaped us into the people we are today. Our stories are powerful, and by sharing them, we can heal not only ourselves but those around us.

"And above all, watch with glittering eyes the whole world around you because the greatest secrets are always hidden in the most unlikely places. Those who don't believe in magic will never find it."

—ROALD DAHL

CHAPTER 7:

THE INFINITE BALANCING ACT

———

"Parts of my life are finally grounded, parts are still wildly up in the air, parts are in flames, and parts are in ashes, yet somehow I'm thriving."

My life has changed immensely since this early morning journal entry, and yet, I still very much relate to these sentiments. Even though I've come so far, I still feel as though I have a long journey ahead. I still have dragons to slay and land to conquer.

Finding this state of equilibrium can sometimes feel like a balancing act. One minute you're high above the crowd, gliding across the trapeze with total ease. The next thing you know, you're nearly falling into the abyss. As your life flashes before your eyes and you fear the worst, you must recenter yourself and find your balance once again. Take one step at a time.

"A well-developed sense of humor is the pole that adds balance to your step as you walk the tightrope of life."

—WILLIAM A. WARD

THE CRITIC WITHIN

According to the National Science Foundation and *Psychology Today* (2017), the average human has approximately 12,000 to 60,000 thoughts per day. Of those thoughts, 80 percent are negative.

Within each of us is a critic, some harsher than others. This little voice has a large influence on every aspect of our lives. This voice can either build you up and make you feel invincible or tear you down, making you want to hide under a rock. Choose to feed this little critic with positivity, compassion, and reassurance. Show yourself mercy rather than placing blame, shame, or guilt on yourself.

Self-talk is extremely important, but the way you choose to talk to yourself is even more crucial to your well-being. People who find themselves regularly engaging in negative self-talk tend to be more stressed (Scott, 2020). Relieve yourself of the pressures and stress that you and others place on you. Make it a priority to take care of your mental, physical, and emotional well-being first.

"Anything that's human is mentionable, and anything that is mentionable can be more manageable. When we can talk about our feelings, they become less overwhelming, less upsetting, and less scary."

—FRED ROGERS

As a society, we often want to give the illusion that we're "okay." Often, we're not okay, but we're afraid others will judge us for not having our shit together. If you ask me, that's completely unfair. Why should it be expected to have your life, your emotions, and your thoughts sorted or "together" at every given moment? Why is it frowned upon to be unsure or lost? Maybe you're not even lost. You're just doing the best you can to manage everything going on in your life without letting it swallow you whole. Most of which the outside world has no recollection of because they can't physically see it. Therefore, toss those ideas out the window. Everyone wears a mask. Choose to take on the world barefaced with a smile. You will find your way, and you will find your balance.

KEEP MOVING, KEEP BREATHING

To say I load a lot onto my plate would be an understatement. I'm aware that I naturally spread myself too thin. I'm a gal with more passions than she can count who likes to stay busy. However, constantly keeping myself overloaded with things to do can result in me becoming quite overwhelmed from time to time. I'm still trying to discover the right balance with my time management.

Even when prioritizing and maximizing my time and efforts throughout the day, sometimes there's still more I want to do or wish I could have gotten to. Then again, I don't think I've ever been truly bored in my life. Even when I've gotten everything done and have nothing pressing on my agenda, I try to research and expand on my knowledge. Not only am I abundantly curious, but I'm always striving to find better ways to balance myself, my time, and my efforts in a means to improve myself, my happiness, and my productivity.

"Life is like riding a bicycle. To keep your balance, you must keep moving."

—ALBERT EINSTEIN

When I'm feeling overwhelmed, minutes away from falling off that bicycle, I have to step back and look at things more objectively. I have to stop what I'm doing, take a deep breath, and regroup. You have to focus on the moving parts that you do have control of. Even when you're walking through the flames, no end in sight, I believe you have complete control over the following:

YOUR MINDSET AND ATTITUDE

More than half the time, it's all in the way you choose to view a situation. You're allowed to be off-balance. You're allowed to be lost. You're allowed to take your time to figure things out. You're allowed to fail. Guess what? Even if you fall flat on your ass, you have the strength to pick yourself up and the courage to start over again. Your thoughts can be crippling, especially when you're down and out. The way you talk to yourself is extremely impactful on your mood, attitude, and mindset. Choose to show yourself love, patience, and grace. Give yourself time to sort things out. Be patient with yourself, for you are not perfect, and just in case you forgot, nobody else is either.

"You need to learn how to select your thoughts just the same way you select your clothes every day. This is a power you can cultivate. If you want to control things in your life so bad, work on the mind. That's the only thing you should be trying to control."

—ELIZABETH GILBERT

Elizabeth Gilbert is an American journalist and best-selling author. She is best known for her memoir, *Eat Pray Love,* published in 2006. Gilbert has written a total of ten novels, but *Eat Pray Love* shortly became an international sensation and a cultural phenomenon. After selling over twelve million copies worldwide and translating it into over thirty different languages, it was made into a movie in 2010 starring Julia Roberts. Elizabeth Gilbert soon became known as "one of the hundred most influential people in the world," according to *TIME* magazine.

The first time I watched *Eat Pray Love*, it moved me. There was one quote that struck a chord with me.

"Ruin is a gift. Ruin is the road to transformation."

—ELIZABETH GILBERT, *EAT PRAY LOVE*

Choosing to view our struggles, challenges, and troubles as transformative is essential. Your journey is an ongoing process, and there are no limits to your growth. Therefore, adjusting your mindset and attitude accordingly is helpful.

In a recent TEDx Talk with Elizabeth Gilbert, Chris Anderson, and Helen Walters, they discussed topics like anxiety, curiosity, loneliness, creativity, procrastination, grief, connection, and hope during a global pandemic (2020). Gilbert speaks about this "paradox" of the human emotional landscape. She explains that although humans are easily the most anxious species, we are also the most capable, resourceful, and resilient species that has ever lived on earth (TED, 2020). Believing you are capable, resilient, and strong enough to get through anything is half the battle. Reframing your thinking to view your journey of growth as gradual is necessary. You can't expect immediate results or instant success. Good things take time. Balance takes time!

"If you don't like something, change it. If you can't change it, change your attitude."

—MAYA ANGELOU

YOUR TIME AND EFFORT

You have full control over the amount of time and effort you exert. If you need to reevaluate and shift your priorities, do it. There's no one-size-fits-all or "right" way to resolve this type of conflict. Help yourself first. If you can't help yourself, you can't help others around you. If you need additional help from others, don't be afraid to ask for it. This is where having a good support system comes in handy.

In 2018, *Forbes* published an article by John Rampton (2018) outlining twenty powerful time management tips. Here are a few that I want to highlight:

1. Set a time limit for each task.

This will help to eliminate distraction and procrastination, keeping you engaged and on task. In my experience, using the Pomodoro Method has been life-changing. This technique consists of twenty-five-minute work intervals, followed by short five-minute breaks. It's a wonderful time management strategy to boost productivity and focus and can be especially beneficial for those with ADHD (Tabackman, 2021).

2. Use a to-do list, but don't abandon tasks.

Creating a detailed to-do list of things that need to be accomplished is extremely helpful. There are obviously times where life or other interruptions will occur; make a note to go back and complete abandoned tasks later.

3. Leave a buffer time between tasks and meetings.

Rampton explains how jumping from task to task without a break may actually have a negative effect. Instead, scheduling buffer time can help you stay more focused and more motivated. "We need time to clear our minds and recharge by going for a walk, meditating, or just daydreaming" (Rampton, 2018).

4. Just say "No."

Learning to say no and creating boundaries for yourself is extremely important. If you already have a jam-packed schedule for the day, it's okay to decline a dinner invitation or help out a friend. Those who are actually your friends won't be upset. You can only handle or take on so much. A friend or loved one will respect that.

Use an online calendar.

Using tools that help you stay organized is essential for time management. Rampton suggests using applications like Google Calendar, Outlook, or Apple Calendar to organize and manage your time better.

"Continuous effort—not strength or intelligence—is the key to unlocking our potential."

—WINSTON CHURCHILL

WELLNESS

Two crucial ways to practice wellness are through the environment we place ourselves in and how we choose to care for ourselves within that environment.

According to the National Counseling Society (2021), the environment in which we live our day-to-day lives is arguably one of the biggest factors contributing to mental health.

The *physical factors* of environmental impact on mental health include sleep deprivation, environmental pollution, hazardous working conditions, extreme weather conditions, smoking, and inaccessible architecture.

The *social factors* of environmental impact on mental health include stigma, discord, abuse, poverty, lack of social support, toxic relationships, and lack of safety (NCS, 2021). As I will be covering most of these in a later chapter, I'd like to focus on stigma. Experiencing stigmas such as racism, sexism, homophobia, or any other form of prejudice increases a person's risk of mental illness (NCS, 2021). When people feel judged, unwelcome, or outcasted in an environment, they tend to turn to avoidance. Nobody wants to go somewhere where they aren't wanted. Let go of bias and choose to treat everyone fairly. The golden rule hasn't been forgotten, but people have become complacent. This isn't an excuse. Welcome and love everyone regardless of who they are. You, as a human being, are not any better than anyone else. Get off your high horse and choose to be more inclusive. Your actions and words are affecting others' mental health. Choose to spread kindness, forgiveness, and love to *all* of your neighbors.

Other factors of your environment that may be causing strain on your mental health include a lack of access to green spaces, lack of visual stimulation, and "oppressive untidiness" (NCS, 2021). It's no secret that beautiful places are not only amazing to look at, but they have a positive effect on your mental health. Get outside and take in the fresh air once in a while. Additionally, living and working in a clean and organized space is essential for your mental well-being. If you are someone who struggles with this and often occupies a messy space, you're causing yourself more anxiety. Personally, I have seen the impact "oppressive untidiness" has on my mental health, productivity, and happiness. Being a tad OCD, I very much enjoy and thrive in a clean space. Clutter in my world means confusion. Eliminating clutter and disorganization helps me function more efficiently.

SELF-CARE

Taking care of yourself or taking time out of your day to show yourself love is more important than you may think. Many people view self-care, or self-love, as a luxury, but in fact, it is essential to your physical, emotional, and mental well-being. One of my absolute favorite forms of self-care is taking a bath. When I've had a long, mentally draining day, I love to put on a face mask, get in the bath, and just unwind. Sometimes I'll listen to a podcast, crack open a book, or watch Netflix. Other times, I'll simply soak in my thoughts. It's important to show yourself this type of care every now and then. Discover what works best for you. Find what puts you most at ease. This mental reset is absolutely needed.

"Self-care is how you take your power back."

—LALAH DELIA

BALANCING THE STRUGGLE

When balancing everything in your life, it can often feel like you don't have enough hands to juggle everything. In an article published by *Psychology Today* (2014), F. Diane Barth outlines five ways to find balance in your life. She is a psychotherapist and psychoanalyst in private practice in New York City.

She begins by talking about transitions in life. She explains that when the seasons change, we are more likely to feel off-balance, specifically mentioning the months of September and June. She also takes a moment to bring forth the idea that the "struggle to find balance" isn't just between work and play in today's high speed, high pressure, and high-stress world (Barth, 2014). The struggle is more complex, lying between your needs and the needs of everyone around you. She gives the example of stay-at-home mothers and the differing struggle they have just to find time to crack open a book or simply be alone. Regardless of the life you lead, there's always a struggle and some area of your life that needs balancing.

FIRST SUGGESTION—MINDSET

Diane's first suggestion has to do with mindset, something we've talked about quite a bit in this chapter. She explains that "balance is not a final goal, but an ongoing process." She says rather than attempting to stay continuously balanced, practice the act of balancing over and over again. You can't be cool, calm, and collected all the time. However, you can be prepared for when you become off-balance.

SECOND SUGGESTION—PRIORITIZING

"In order to stay on course, you may have to reexamine your priorities regularly." I think this is wonderful advice from Diane. This is something I have to do on a weekly basis, if not daily. I'm constantly reevaluating what is most important at any given moment so I can realign my time and efforts.

THIRD SUGGESTION—LONG—AND SHORT-TERM GOALS

Diane urges us to set both long—and short-term goals. She refers to a term used in business called "Tactics and Strategy." The strategy represents the long-term goal, or bigger picture, while the tactics are a sum of short-term goals to help you achieve your long-term goal. Therefore, remind yourself that you must take small steps to complete larger ones.

FOURTH SUGGESTION—BE SPECIFIC

Diane Barth suggests being more specific. She talks about quality time and health goals, explaining that setting goals is one thing, but if you're not specific with them, "it's hard to know whether or not you've accomplished that goal," making it harder to truly feel balanced.

FIFTH SUGGESTION—SUPPORT

This last suggestion relates closely to my experiences. Diane stresses the importance of support from others. She explains that it's often easier to balance with another person. Having a support system of people that are willing to help you when needed, offer guidance and support, as well as keep you accountable is a must.

FIND PEACE IN THE PROCESS OF BECOMING

"Moderate in order to taste the joys of life in abundance."

—EPICURUS

The key takeaway from this chapter is switching your mindset to view balance as an ongoing process rather than an impossible destination. It's about making the choice to constantly reevaluate and strategize for the time at hand. You may never achieve this perfect place you've envisioned, but you will transform as a human being. Find peace in the process. Find peace in the journey of life. Finding that rhythm and harmony is a continuous process. It boils down to being honest with yourself, putting forth your best effort, and accepting your dysfunction sometimes. It's not always going to be easy, and things are certainly not always going to go the way you planned. A lot of the time, life and all of its moving parts are going to be messy. Learn not to sweat the small stuff.

Whether you are a student, a parent, or just a human being trying to make it in this world, give yourself a pat on the back. You made it through the day. You're still breathing. Tomorrow is a new day filled with opportunity and growth if you so choose to chase it. Go forth and conquer!

PART 3:

I HOPE
YOU DANCE

I HOPE YOU DANCE

———

"I hope you never lose your sense of wonder,
You get your fill to eat but always keep that hunger,
May you never take one single breath for granted,
God forbid love ever leave you empty-handed,
I hope you still feel small when you stand beside the ocean,
Whenever one door closes, I hope one more opens,
Promise me that you'll give faith a fighting chance,
And when you get the choice to sit it out or dance.
I hope you dance..."

—LEE ANN WOMACK

Dear Reader,

I'm proud of you. You've come a long way from where you first started.

Yet, your journey is far from over. I think the hardest part about anything in life is taking that leap; fully surrendering your fear in pursuit of the things that set your soul on fire.

You can prepare for it all you want, but the truth is, it's not going to make the jump any less terrifying.

A few months ago, I moved across the country. I packed up everything I've ever owned, gathered the essentials, and took a chance, hoping to land on my feet. In my travels, I stopped in this quaint coffee shop somewhere north of Dallas. While sipping a latte and attempting (keyword: attempting) to cure my writer's block, I overheard a conversation between two women that struck a chord with me.

One woman shared her anxiety and apprehension about attaining goals in her future, while the other simply looked at her. This confident, collected woman paused and softly smiled before saying, "There is no guarantee of anything in life, just trust. Trust that everything will work out the way it's meant to."

Really let that one sink in. If nothing in life is guaranteed, why do we spend so much time dwelling and deliberating in fear before making strides toward the things we want most out of life?

Fear is the thief of faith and trust. When we allow fear, or anxiety, to start dictating our perception of the world or, even worse, our actions—we no longer have faith that the universe that surrounds us works in our favor.

Just like any healthy relationship, there is nothing without trust. As you head into this last section of my book, have trust in the process.

In this last section, I will cover:

- Owning your dysfunction!
- How to find your purpose and share your light with others.
- Maintaining your growth over time.
- Everything you need to know about happiness and satisfaction.
- Embracing the journey of personal growth at every stage of life.

You're on your way to a better version of yourself. Trust me, the struggle is always worth it in the end. As you continue on, remember to find joy in your imperfections, your failures, and your progress. Life is too short to wait. I hope you choose to wake up each day and dance in all life has to offer.

With love,
R

CHAPTER 8

OWNING YOUR
DYSFUNCTION

———

"Perfectionism is internalized oppression."

—GLORIA STEINEM

I can't recall what my defining moment was, but from a young age, I've struggled with the idea of perfection. One could say I'm a *recovering perfectionist.*

Creative and fine arts spoke to me from an early age. I was practically singing and dancing before I could confidently recite my ABCs. Therefore, it wasn't a surprise when my parents made the executive decision to put me in dance classes.

From the moment my feet touched the silky studio floor, I was in heaven. The studio became my sanctuary. I found my voice, my confidence, my strengths, and even my weaknesses within those four walls. The love I found began to radiate from within. The adrenaline rush of performance brought out an alter ego;

a fierce yet delicate being that allowed others to bear witness to her most vulnerable self, leaving everything on the stage.

Expressing myself through movement quickly became second nature. When I felt overwhelmed or stressed, I turned to dance. When I felt happy and hopeful, song and dance poured from my soul. Dance has been there for me when it felt like nobody else was. Dance has been there to ground me, catch me, and hold me tight when it felt like my world was crumbling beneath my feet. When the world attempted to swallow me whole, dance helped carefully piece my broken pieces back together.

Things didn't always come naturally, though. Music may run through my veins, but when it came to technical skills, I often had to put in extensive work. Given this, I learned to naturally seek validation from my teachers and mentors, sometimes letting their perspective and judgment dictate what was right or wrong. Soon, their eyes began to dictate what was beautiful and ugly in my world. Like clay to a sculptor, I became malleable in their hands, easily molded by their directions and critiques. While this adaptability to fulfill their creative vision was essential in a classroom setting, I allowed it to seep into other areas of my life. Without even realizing it, I began to examine myself and every move I made under a harsh spotlight. Slowly but surely, I became my toughest critic.

"I put my heart and soul into my work and have lost my mind in the process."

—VINCENT VAN GOGH

Born in 1853, Vincent Van Gogh led anything but an ordinary life (Biography, 2020). As the eldest child of six and named after his parents' stillborn baby, he experienced lifelong resentment, disapproval, and minimal affection from his mother. At the young age of fifteen, his parents removed him from school to work due to their financial instability. Fortunately, he was sent to work with his uncle Cornelius, who owned an art dealership, Goupil & Cie (Biogrpahics, 2020). It wasn't long until Vincent was fluent in French, German, English, and his native language, Dutch. Through his work experiences, he discovered a love for English culture, art galleries, and Charles Dickens (Biogrpahics, 2020).

Buckle up, friends. This is where it gets interesting. After falling in love, being rejected, attempting to become a minister, developing a wildly inappropriate love for absinthe, cutting his own ear off, and being diagnosed with Syphilis and Gonorrhea, Vincent landed himself in two different mental institutions (Biography, 2020). In the second asylum, his brother Theo financially ensured he had two separate quarters; one for living and one for his art. Van Gogh eventually was well enough to live on his own again, but it wasn't long before his mental health plummeted. He struggled with self-hatred, thinking he was a burden and that the world would be a better place without him. Shortly after, Van Gogh attempted to take his own life. Although he wasn't successful, he did later die as a result of that gunshot wound.

"There is no perfection, only beautiful versions of brokenness."

—SHANNON L. ALDER

The story of Vincent Van Gogh is one that moves me to tears. Vincent was plagued with mental illness, so much so that it eventually killed him at the mere age of thirty-seven (Biography, 2020). He experienced immense hardship, he received little to no support or praise, and he hadn't the slightest clue how talented he was. He spent his life transforming his passion and pain into post-impressionist beauty. Today, Vincent Van Gogh is one of the world's greatest artists. The Starry Night, his most notable work, is worth approximately $100 million (Paintona, 2021). With no formal training, this tortured yet passionate man painted some of the most valuable and beloved works, those of which greatly influenced twentieth-century art. Yet, he was utterly blind to his greatness.

Now and forevermore, I want you to remember something, reader. Just like failure, your dysfunction is not fatal, not if you refuse to give it the power to be. Don't you dare let anyone convince you that you are worthless because of the baggage you may carry. Does Van Gogh's painful baggage make him less of a creative genius? Does it take away from his legacy? Absolutely not. If anything, it makes him more relatable. It makes him human, just like the rest of us.

"Your darkest moments are not meant to be swept under the carpet, hidden from the world in the silent pursuit of perfection. The darkness you've overcome is your ticket into leadership. It's what you're meant to light up in the world."

—VIRONIKA TUGALEVA

LET'S TALK INSECURITIES

"He often felt that too many people lived their lives acting and pretending, wearing masks, and losing themselves in the process."

—NICHOLAS SPARKS

Everyone wears a mask; you, your neighbor, even your closest confidant at times. Each day, we wake up and put on a mask before taking on the outside world.

It's just like putting on makeup. With each dab of concealer and each swipe of powdery perfection, we conceal our baggage and highlight our best assets. We spend minutes and sometimes hours blurring and minimizing the appearance of imperfections, hoping no one sees through our careful disguise. We paint on a new, "flawless" face praying others become blind to the conflict that resides beneath the surface, praying they can't see our most vulnerable parts.

"Behind every mask, there is a face, and behind that, a story."

—MARTY RUBIN

What's under the mask, though? Isn't that what we all wonder as we strut around each other pretending to be "perfect"? The meticulously calculated disguise we wear each day is in an effort to conceal our fears, insecurities, secrets, and weaknesses from our peers. The fear of judgment and the shame of imperfection dawns upon us all in some form.

Whether it's the face you paint on each morning or the choices you make each day, we've all betrayed ourselves at some point; in an effort to feel more accepted, loved, admired, or praised. Let's face it, we're either scraping pennies or the inside of a foundation tube just to prove our worthiness to someone else.

Do you spend that kind of time and effort proving it to yourself, though?

Allow me to pose some questions:

- What are we so afraid of?
- Why are we so concerned with what others think about us?
- If we all have skeletons in the closet, why are we hiding from each other?
- Wouldn't it be easier to collectively expose these skeletons, make peace with them, and live among them? To dance with them rather than around them?
- Are we truly incapable of accepting imperfection?
- Aren't human beings imperfect in nature?

I challenge you to make peace with your demons and set them free. I challenge you to peel back some of those layers and show the world what's under your mask. Let others see your face, the one you try so hard to conceal. Authenticity is beautiful, and so are you; imperfections included.

The truth is, we're all a little broken, a little insecure, and a little scared. We all have doubts and worries. We worry that we won't be "good enough" or worthy of our wildest dreams. Yet, hiding doesn't make us feel any better. In fact, most of the time, it makes us feel worse. That baggage silently weighs us down, slowly but surely bringing us closer and closer to drowning in the depths of our own dysfunction. Self-talk doesn't have to feel like a flesh-eating bacterium. Your demons only have the power to eat you alive if you give them the power to. You are in control. You hold the power here.

I challenge you to choose vulnerability, for it will set you free. Let those skeletons out of the closet!

"An exciting and inspiring future awaits you beyond the noise in your mind, beyond the guilt, doubt, fear, shame, insecurity, and heaviness of the past you carry around."

—DEBBIE FORD

COMPARISON: THE INSTANT MOOD-KILLER

"Can you remember who you were before the world told you who you should be?"

—DANIELLE LAPORTE

Genuinely, step back and ask yourself this. Can you remember?

For the longest time, I too, forgot. I abandoned that creative little girl and chose to nurture a watered-down version of who the world and my peers thought I should be. I continuously felt I had to dim my light so others could shine.

"Comparison is the thief of joy."

—THEODORE ROOSEVELT

You are not like any other being. You are unique; your own individual creation. So, riddle me this:

- How can you logically compare yourself to someone else?
- Is it benefiting you in any way?
- Does comparing yourself make you feel good? Does it make you feel happier?

Forget comparing your physical appearance to another person; that's an entirely separate issue in itself. However, comparing your life, growth, and accomplishments to another person is even more detrimental to the individual. This can be harmful to our mental, emotional, and even physical health. We look at our life, then at other people's growth, and suddenly our progress and accomplishments don't matter. Why should that be? Your little victories, your failures, your growth *matters*. You are not on the same playing field as your peers. You are on your own path, traveling at your own pace. There's no set pace or speed limit you need to be traveling at. You'll get to where you need to be. Why rush the process and miss out on valuable lessons?

"When the product is yourself, it becomes harder and harder to sleep at night."
—CATHERINE REITMAN

Catherine Reitman is an American actress, writer, and producer. She is the "showrunner" of her own series, *Workin' Moms* (TEDx Talks, 2017). As the daughter of Ivan Reitman, a forefather of comedy and the mastermind behind Ghostbusters, she naturally fell into acting. However, after years of trying to be the "perfect fit" for someone else's character, she eventually felt like she didn't have control or say in her own career. Catherine turned to writing. She describes this transition as feeling illegal, "like writing was meant for someone smarter than me, or more special than me" (TEDx Talks, 2017). She tells a story about an early idea of hers, to which her blunt father told her to "leave that to Aaron Sorkin." She discusses the shame she felt for stepping outside of her comfort zone.

In Catherine's TEDx Talk, she discusses insights from author and palliative care nurse Bronnie Ware. In Ware's book, published in 2011, she shares the five biggest regrets of people on their death bed. According to Ware (2021), the number one regret is, "I wish I'd had the courage to live a life true to myself, not the life others expected of me." For Catherine, this was her wake-up call to listen to her inner voice. While her father may have been spot-on about her premature, medical dramedy pitch, she asserts that: "Aaron Sorkin didn't become Aaron Sorkin by allowing anyone who did something before him halt his development" (TEDx Talks, 2017).

Catherine did end up listening to that inner voice and finally chasing her truest self. We can't simply sit back and live in the shadows of those we look up to; we must rise up to the challenge. Her experience with postpartum depression and authentic depiction of life as a working mother led her to write her own television series, which is hilariously relatable if you've never seen it. The show does an excellent job of discussing taboo topics and harsher realities that go un-touched within motherhood and parenting. Catherine gives two pieces of advice to those flirting with the choice to take that challenge:

1. It's a lot of work.
2. That work has to be specific to you.

"You must cut your voice so sharply that it can be mistaken for nobody but you."

—CATHERINE REITMAN

Choosing to say "yes," and genuinely believe in ourselves is difficult. Being true to oneself and chasing our deepest desires is petrifying. However, if you were to sit around comparing yourself to those successful in your craft, how far would that get you?

Comparison can be the thief of joy, having a plethora of negative side effects, but what if we were able to use it to our advantage?

TIP-TOEING THE LINE: DANGERS AND POTENTIAL BENEFITS OF COMPARISON

Comparison can be dangerous if we allow our thoughts to acknowledge no bounds. Some negative side effects may include resentment, anxiety, low self-esteem, lack of confidence, depression, and much more. According to Do Something, a youth-led organization combating social change and civic action:

- Seven in ten girls believe that they are not good enough or don't measure up in some way, including their looks, performance in school and relationships with friends and family members.
- About 20 percent of teens will experience depression before they even reach adulthood.

Comparison to our peers can be debilitating, but if we choose to redirect it—it can motivate us. Like Catherine Reitman's story, maybe it's simply a call to rise up to the challenge.

"No one can make you feel inferior without your consent."

—ELEANOR ROOSEVELT

WHAT DOES IT MEAN TO OWN YOUR DYSFUNCTION?

"Beauty begins the moment you decide to be yourself."

—COCO CHANEL

Each and every one of us has something that is faulty, impaired, abnormal, or unhealthy—whether it be a personality trait, insecurity, bad habit, or addiction.

Owning your dysfunction means objectively *identifying* those dark parts, compassionately *evaluating* them, and *accepting* them despite the opinions of the peanut gallery.

Taking ownership of these things puts you in the driver's seat. You're the only one who can determine how heavy that baggage is. Are you going to let it weigh you down and crush your spirit? Or are you going to throw that shit out the window and live your life on your terms? It's about standing confidently in those flaws and loving yourself in spite of them.

Owning your dysfunction feels like coming up for fresh air, midnight drives with the windows down and the kind of heartfelt laugh that follows a really good cry. Nobody wants to admit they're fucked up. Why would they? But if you don't, you leave room for everyone else to stick their two cents in.

For me, owning my dysfunction looked like finally admitting that my life didn't look like other people's; I didn't look the same, I didn't think the same, I didn't act the same, and my life sure as hell didn't feel the same. Standing in my dysfunction, or vulnerability, looked like accepting my bad days, having the courage to ask for help, confiding in loved ones about my struggles, and knowing that none of it made me less worthy. Owning my dysfunction was like giving my inner child the big hug she's been deserving of for years after I'd shamed, guilted, and bashed her for her imperfections.

"Vulnerability is the birthplace of innovation, creativity, and change."

—BRENÉ BROWN

I'm not sure there are enough words in the English dictionary to encompass all that is Brené Brown. But here's my weak attempt.

Dr. Brené Brown is a researcher, storyteller, and Texan at heart. She's a research professor at the University of Houston, where she holds the Huffington Foundation Endowed Chair at The Graduate College of Social Work (Brown, 2021). She's spent decades studying vulnerability, shame, empathy, and courage. She also happens to be the author of five number-one *New York Times* bestsellers and a podcast host. Her TEDx Talk, The Power of Vulnerability, is one of the most viewed in the world, with over fifty million views (Brown, 2021).

In this TEDx Talk (2011), Brené thoroughly breaks down the concept of vulnerability. From her research to her own personal struggles, she came to similar findings. In response to struggling with whole-hearted vulnerability, she concludes that we do the following:

1. We numb.
2. We make the uncertain certain.
3. We perfect.
4. We pretend.

We do everything *except* stand in our dysfunction. We'll numb, deflect, or play pretend before we simply own our struggle. Brené encourages us to let ourselves be deeply seen and believe that we're enough.

"Vulnerability sounds like truth and feels like courage. Truth and courage aren't always comfortable, but they're never weakness."

—BRENÉ BROWN

Given, sometimes the expectation isn't to be "perfect" or always have your shit together. Sometimes, you're the only one putting that pressure on yourself. Take a step back and show yourself mercy. Show yourself love. You have flaws, dysfunctional behaviors, and things you may not like about yourself. Everyone has things they'd like to change. That is okay!

Own that dysfunction. Own your differences. Your power in life is those differences. You are not like anyone else; that is your superpower. So, *own it.* Stop trying to fit into a mold or follow someone else's plan. Determine what you like, what you want, who you are, what you need, and what works best for *you.*

FREEDOM: THE BITTERSWEET TRUTH
ABOUT ACCEPTANCE

"Imperfection is beauty, madness is genius, and it's better to be absolutely ridiculous than absolutely boring."

—MARILYN MONROE

Not one singular human being is perfect, yet we strive for the impossible. We create unreasonable expectations and then nearly kill ourselves trying to meet them. When we don't meet these goals and expectations, we then compare ourselves to other people and then let those comparisons determine how we feel about ourselves. This is a toxic cycle. One that must come to an end.

It's time, friends. It's time to unpack our baggage, process it, and accept it for all of its loveliest, ugliest and messy parts. You're not damaged, or broken, or unlovable. You're human. There's a newfound freedom that comes from releasing the mental anguish we place on ourselves. We're so worried about what others will think or how our accomplishments measure up that we forget to gaze at the bigger picture. We forget to admire how extraordinary we are.

"What if I fall? Oh, but my darling, what if you fly?"

—ERIN HANSON

CHAPTER 9

THE LIGHT
FROM WITHIN

"The two most important days in your life are the day you are born, and the day you find out why."

—MARK TWAIN

When my mother was pregnant with me, she frequently had strangers approach her in public. They'd ask to touch her stomach and tell her I was an old soul, or they felt how special I was. Some would even tell her I'd "been here before." While many of you may be thinking that's absolutely insane, I think it's actually quite fascinating.

From a very young age, I've known my purpose in life was to help, love, and connect with other people. I knew I was meant to spread my passion, heart, and voice with others in some capacity. I just hadn't imagined it would be through my writing until this year. If you had told me I'd write a book years ago, I probably would have told you to keep dreaming.

I would have laughed, not because I thought I was incapable, but because very few people actually accomplish it.

Throughout this process, others have consistently reminded me *only 2 percent* of people that begin writing a book ever finish (Koester, 2019). Hell, there have been many times when I've questioned whether I had the talent and rigor to be a part of that 2 percent. For some perspective, that's less than the percentage of students who get accepted into Harvard each year. Last fall, Harvard University had an acceptance rate of 4.6 percent (Acceptance Rate, 2021). So, if you're holding my words in your hands right now, I've successfully defied the odds.

"There is no greater gift you can give or receive than to honor your calling. It's why you were born. And how you become most truly alive."

—OPRAH WINFREY

I believe our souls come into this life with a purpose and a meaning, even if we have to spend our entire existence figuring it out—which can be a purpose in and of itself. But, nonetheless, you are here for a reason. You have a purpose and reason for being. Life would be meaningless if you didn't.

So, what's yours?

What is your purpose?

Along the beaten path, I've stumbled upon a few different philosophies that I find fascinating. While each of us has our own set of values and priorities, alternative routes may be required to reach our final, desired destination. The following ideologies may help you discover your path and help define what you should focus on in your search for purpose.

LOGOTHERAPY: NATURAL SEEKERS OF MEANING

"Everything can be taken from a man but one thing: the last of the human freedoms—to choose one's attitude in any given set of circumstances, to choose one's own way."

—VIKTOR E. FRANKL

Viktor Emil Frankl was an Austrian neurologist, psychiatrist, philosopher, psychotherapist, author, and Holocaust survivor (Britannica, 2021). In his lifetime, Dr. Frankl published a total of thirty-nine books. Among these, the most notable is his best-selling book, *Man's Search For Meaning* (1984), a memoir based upon his real-life experiences in Nazi concentration camps. To which this psychological genius supposedly wrote over the course of only nine days.

Dr. Frankl became interested in psychology early on in life, particularly fascinated with depression and suicide (Britannica, 2021). So it came as no surprise when he later developed a school of psychotherapy known as logotherapy. Frankl's work is considered the "third school" of Viennese psychotherapy among well-known psychologists like Sigmund Freud and Alfred Adler. Sigmund Freud believed humans were driven by pleasure, while Alfred Adler thought humans were primarily driven by power. Unlike these two, Victor Frankl believed in the pursuit of meaning rather than "in the mere gratification and satisfaction of drives and instincts" (Academy of Ideas, 2016). He believed that humans are motivated to seek meaning, found uniquely in each of our lives, and actually argued that "when a man cannot find meaning, he numbs himself with pleasure" (McLeod, 2021). Furthermore, I would argue, isn't there meaning to be found in power and pleasure?

"I am convinced that in the final analysis, there is no situation that does not contain within it the seed of a meaning."

—VIKTOR FRANKL

Dr. Frankl believed there were three ways to discover meaning in life.

1. Through Action
2. Through Love
3. Through Suffering

From work to relationships, and even the traumatic experiences we may come face-to-face with along our journey— there is meaning to be found.

THE STRUGGLE IS REAL: BREAKING OUT OF THE EXISTENTIAL VACUUM

"Between stimulus and response, there is a space. In that space is our power to choose our response. In our response lies our growth and our freedom."

—VIKTOR FRANKL

In Viktor Frankl's research, he discovered a twentieth-century phenomenon that he referred to as the "existential vacuum." He believed the loss of tradition and animal instinct within humans brought boredom, which led to this idea of a meaningless life. He explains, "no instinct tells him what he has to do, and no tradition tells him what he ought to do; sometimes he does not even know what he wishes to do" (Academy of Ideas, 2016). Conformism and totalitarianism can result from this; one either wishes to do what everyone else is doing or does as other people want of them. Sense of self, or inner direction, goes right out the window. We see this concept in society today. There is an intense pressure toward conformity but a lack of meaning in people's day-to-day lives. Dr. Frankl went further to hypothesize this phenomenon was partially to blame for the mass neurotic triad: depression, aggression, and addiction. He drew these observations and conclusions after the Second World War. If Viktor Frankl was alive today, I'm sure he'd have a bone to pick.

"I think it's because we're looking for the meaning. Where is the meaning? We have mindless jobs, we take frantic vacations, deficit finance trips to the mall to buy more things that we think are going to fill these holes in our lives. Is it any wonder that we've lost our sense of direction?"

—MATTHEW MCCONAUGHEY

So, how can we practice logotherapy as a means to break away from this existential vacuum? How do we avoid the triad?

Three Practices to Implement: (Cuncic, 2021)

1. Dereflection

Dereflection is a practice aimed to help shift your focus away from yourself and toward others in a means to combat hyper-reflection or overanalyzing.

2. Paradoxical Intention

This is a technique sometimes suggested in the case of anxiety or phobia, where fear can be paralyzing. To combat that fear, this technique embraces directly facing the things that terrify you most.

3. Socratic Dialogue

Socratic dialogue can be described as a tool used to aid self-discovery by noticing and interpreting your own words. Having a therapist listen to your thoughts, detect patterns, and help to dissect the meaning within them can be highly impactful.

Utilizing such practices can keep us grounded and in tune with ourselves so that we don't lose our way and get sucked into this existential vacuum.

IKIGAI: FINDING YOUR PURPOSE

"A happy man is too satisfied with the present to dwell too much on the future."

—ALBERT EINSTEIN

In Japan, it is said that the secret to a "longer, happier, and more fulfilled life can be summed up in one word: ikigai" (Mogi, 2019). Ikigai is a concept with no direct English translation that embodies "a reason for being" or the reason why you get out of bed each morning. This age-old ideology originated in Okinawa, Japan. Okinawa is not only the birthplace of karate but home to the highest percent of centenarians in the world (Mogi, 2019). This word embodies not only happiness but purpose within the daily life each of us leads.

In an article by BBC (2017), Yukari Mitsuhashi explains that "Japanese people believe that the sum of small joys in everyday life results in more fulfilling life as a whole." The concept of ikigai embraces just this and can be associated with the nation's long life expectancy. Here in the United States, the average life expectancy for women is eighty-one years and seventy-six years for men. Whereas in Japan, the average life expectancy is at an all-time high where women live eighty-seven years, and men live approximately eighty-one years. What is more impressive is that according to the World Health Organization, NBC, and Business Insider, the Japanese can live seventy-five of those years disability-free and fully healthy.

Is it possible that a life purpose can improve our health?

According to the American Psychosomatic Society, "possessing a high sense of purpose in life is associated with a reduced risk of mortality and cardiovascular disease" (2015).

"Ikigai is the action we take in pursuit of happiness."

—YUKARI MITSUHASHI

I had absolutely no idea what ikigai was until I found myself absently scrolling through TEDx Talks one evening. Prepped with hot, chamomile tea in hand, I randomly selected one by

Tim Tamashiro. Tim is a Canadian jazz singer, speaker, entertainer, and former national radio host. He is also the author of the Amazon best-selling book, *How To Ikigai* (Tamashiro, 2021). In 2018, Tim gave a TEDx Talk about the concept of ikigai and how it can enrich our lives. He describes ikigai, or "life's worth," as a treasure map to finding one's happiness (TEDx Talks, 2018).

This map has four directions:

1. Do what you love.
2. Do what you're good at.
3. Do what the world needs.
4. Do what you can be rewarded for.

I want you to take a moment to identify what these four directions are in your own life. Write them down on a piece of paper... I'll wait. Go make your cup of tea, get comfy, and get to thinking.

We all have dreams that live inside us, but we often forget to ask why. Why do we want such things, and why was that dream planted within us? Don't forget to ask yourself the hard questions.

Ikigai is an action and a verb. One's purpose can be to create, serve, build, heal, connect, and so on. What do you feel called toward, reader? Discovering this is half the battle.

Tim Tamashiro stresses the difference between a job and work. He explains that a "job" is merely a paid position of employment, while "work" is an activity involving mental or physical effort done to achieve a purpose or result (TEDx Talks, 2018). Can these two things be the same thing? Of course, but they aren't always. Many people occupy positions of employment that serve no purpose but to pay their bills and put food on their table. If that's the case, in what areas of our day-to-day do we seek meaning?

Now, before you go quitting your corporate nine to five, read that list again. Your occupation can encompass one or all of those directions. Not everyone is career-oriented. For many, a job can simply be something you get rewarded for. Maybe you have a side hustle or hobby that provides your other directions in life. Fifty percent of millennials have a side hustle (TEDx Talks, 2018). Tim suggests "starting part-time" or taking advantage of the hours outside of that nine to five window that typically gets underutilized. Take time to do what you love, and love what you do, whatever that may be.

In this same evening of TEDx binge-watching, I discovered another talk by Emily Bidle, an eleventh-grade student at the time, speaking about how ikigai is the secret to a purposeful life. She explains that practicing ikigai requires deep experimentation and self-exploration by pursuing concrete actions and reflecting back thoughtfully (TEDx Talks, 2019). In this practice of experimentation and exploration, one can discover how passion, mission, profession, and vocation can intersect and bring more meaning into one's career and life.

Your purpose, or your ikigai, is your light. It's the dream, or the fire, that burns within you. No one can dim that fierce light. No one can take that away from you, for it is divinely yours. So experiment, explore, and then change the world with it!

"The heart of human excellence often begins to beat when you discover a pursuit that absorbs you, frees you, challenges you, or gives you a sense of meaning, joy, or passion."

—TERRY ORLICK

SHARING YOUR LIGHT

Have you ever had one of those surreal concert experiences? You know the one I'm talking about. The one that lights something up inside your soul. Maybe even something you've lost sight of. It's one of those experiences where you walk out of an arena feeling like an entirely different person than who walked in hours before. From the moment the stadium lights dim, butterflies flutter in the depths of your stomach, anticipating the excitement that awaits. You're instantly entranced and disengaged from every worry or trouble that was weighing you down minutes prior. The outside world disappears as you allow yourself to be fully present in the moment. You let yourself feel the energy and the love that surrounds you. This love lifts you up so high that even when the music fades, the smoke clears, the people empty, the screams and echoes die out, and the confetti falls... the energy still fills the room. Have you ever stood in an empty arena after a concert? One can still feel the magic that was once there. You can't un-feel it. You're forever changed.

"I have no desire to save you. I only wish to show you the light that exists within you, so you can save yourself."

—BILLY CHAPATA

This is the feeling I hope to provide others with. I can only hope that the experiences I share with others are meaningful enough that they leave a lasting impact. Even you, reading this right now—I can only hope to leave an impact on your day, let alone your life. I can only hope my words make you feel heard, understood, loved, and accepted. I want others to remember my heart. I couldn't care if they remembered what I wore or what car I drove. I want others to remember how I treated others and who I was as a human being. I want them to remember how I made them *feel*.

"Carve your name on hearts, not tombstones. A legacy is etched into the minds of others and the stories they share about you."

—SHANNON L. ALDER

FROM CONSUMER TO CREATOR

"There is no greater agony than bearing an untold story inside you."

—MAYA ANGELOU

From a young age, I threw myself into any form of story-telling, from books to movies, music, and lengthy conversations with elders. I'm incredibly grateful to have a family full of loud, theatric storytellers. The apple indeed does not fall far from the tree! Think it runs in my Irish-Italian blood?

Although I was fascinated with stories, I never wrote any of my own until middle school. In sixth grade, I was one of three students accepted into an eighth-grade, advanced creative writing class. It was there that I discovered I had a love for writing, yet I struggled to find my voice within my words. Add in a touch of perfectionism, and I put writing on the back burner altogether for a while, deeming it a fulfilling hobby at best.

It was in high school when a therapist I was seeing at the time recommended journaling. Even though she admitted she'd never met a fifteen-year-old so level-headed or self-aware, she encouraged that I give it a try as a form of stress relief. At the time, I brushed off her advice and didn't see the importance. It wasn't until years later, my senior year of high school, that I felt the weight and meaning of her words. One entry of complete gibberish became dozens and thousands of words kept privately in notes. It was not only a fantastic form of stress relief, but I began to understand myself more. I began to accept and love myself more through those unfiltered reflections.

My whole life, I've been a gatekeeper of stories, stories of my own, family, friends, and complete strangers. Yet, I've never shared them out of fear, fear that my words weren't enough. That someone else's perception, voice, and syntax was more impressive or powerful and would overshadow mine. So, I kept them to myself. I wrote for fun. I wrote for me. I wrote to understand myself better. I wrote to express myself. Writing became my personal therapy.

(Thank you, Dr. Caplan... you were right.)

I hadn't ever shared more than a school paper before August 2019, when I started writing articles for an online platform called the Odyssey. Most of which, I played safe. I wrote many lifestyle pieces that somewhat showcased my voice but lacked the true depth I possessed. However, the few pieces that weren't surface level received massive feedback. Whether they were later featured articles or just praised by peers, it blew me away. When I had started to write about things that actually mattered, things that were difficult to discuss, things that were raw and vulnerable, people wanted to hear more. My voice and my experiences had resonated with others. Months later, in February of 2020, Eric Koester reached out to me.

Eric Koester is an award-winning Professor of Entrepreneurship and Innovation at Georgetown University McDonough School of Business. He also happens to be the founder of the Creator Institute.

It turns out, all I really needed was for a complete stranger to believe in me and keep me accountable. Eric Koester did just that and so much more. Saying *yes* to something that scared the living daylights out of me turned out to be one of the greatest adventures I've ever taken. This book, this process, and this monumental time in my life have been transformational in my journey of personal growth and development. I've grown and healed in ways I could have never imagined. This process forced me to dig deep and confront parts of myself I'd been unwilling or unable to before. It's forced me to share parts of myself I may have once been terrified to. It's forced me to let go of my fear of failure or the unknown. Even if nothing were to ever come from these words, this process provided me with greater knowledge, healing, and joy than I could have ever dreamed possible.

"That's the power of the Creator Institute. We empower people to find their purpose, their calling. And facilitate a process for them to discover, learn and create something that demonstrates that purpose. That's the credibility that impacts others—a sign that tells others something special."

—CREATOR INSTITUTE

I don't think I'll ever be able to repay Professor Koester, the Creator Institute, or New Degree Press for this opportunity. Yet, I'm forever grateful and so incredibly excited to see where my purpose takes me in life.

Sometimes we find ourselves on a path we may have never considered, or thought was possible, yet there emerges a better, more enlightened version of self.

"You have brains in your head. You have feet in your shoes. You can steer yourself in any direction you choose. You're on your own. And you know what you know. And you are the one who'll decide where to go..."

—DR. SEUSS, OH, THE PLACES YOU'LL GO!

CHAPTER 10

MAINTAINING YOUR GROWTH

"Wanting something is not enough. You must hunger for it. Your motivation must be absolutely compelling in order to overcome the obstacles that will invariably come your way."

—LES BROWN

Have you ever made a goal, told yourself you're going to take action, and then said, "it's okay, it can wait until tomorrow"?

Better yet, answer this: *When you wake up each morning, do you feel like getting out of bed?*

Discovering your ikigai, or reason for getting out of bed each morning is merely half the battle. Often, we can identify the things we want out of life or what drives us, yet we fail to follow through. We fail to take action, let alone be intentional and consistent with them. We tell ourselves it can wait until tomorrow, but should it?

We commonly tell ourselves that we're going to wake up in the morning and go to the gym, but by the time 6 a.m. rolls around, we're groaning and rolling over to hit the snooze button.

"Hesitation is the kiss of death. You might hesitate for just a nanosecond, but that's all it takes. That one small hesitation triggers a mental system that's designed to stop you. And it happens in less than—you guessed it—five seconds."

—MEL ROBBINS

Our inner snooze button keeps us from achieving our goals, in and outside the bedroom. Every single day, we have ideas capable of changing our life, the world, and the way we feel. Yet, what do we do with those thoughts? We silence them. We hesitate and eventually don't act on them.

Mel Robbins is a best-selling author, radio and TV host, CNN commentator, and motivational speaker. In her TEDx Talk (2011), titled "How to Stop Screwing Yourself Over," she stresses the notion that we are *never* going to feel like it; we are never going to feel like getting up and taking action. In science, this concept is referred to as "activation energy," aka the force or energy needed to initiate a reaction. Hence, if you don't light a fire under your own ass, nobody else is going to. As Mel says, "No one is coming. It is up to you." You must light your own fire, pushing yourself into actions that will produce the things you want in life.

She has a theory that she calls the five-second rule. When these ideas or impulses emerge, if we don't choose to act upon them and activate our energy—we figuratively pull our own emergency brake and kill the idea entirely.

"Even if you are not ready for the day, it cannot always be night."

—GWENDOLYN BROOKS

She explains that getting what you want in life is simple, but it's never going to be easy. You must force yourself to:

1. Get out of your head.
2. Get past your feelings.
3. Get outside your comfort zone.

The magic happens outside of our comfort zone, and it only takes five seconds.

"The 5 Second Rule: The moment you have an instinct to act on a goal, you must 5-4-3-2-1 and physically move or your brain will stop you."

—MEL ROBBINS

Your homework from Mel:

Tomorrow morning, set your alarm thirty minutes earlier than you usually would. When that alarm starts blaring, throw off the covers, and "get your ass up." Get up and go to that early spin class, meditate, journal, caffeinate, execute the plans you originally intended to. Start your day with intention!

"You have been assigned this mountain so that you can show others it can be moved."

—MEL ROBBINS

BELIEVING IN THE POWER OF YET: ALL ABOUT GROWTH MINDSET

"Character, heart, the mind of a champion. It's what makes great athletes, and it's what comes from the growth mindset with its focus on self-development, self-motivation, and responsibility."

—CAROL DWECK

Carol Dweck is an American psychologist and professor at Stanford University. Her work creates a bridge between developmental psychology, social psychology, and personality psychology. She has done extensive research in the field of motivation, why people succeed (or don't), and how to foster success (TED, 2021). Carol examines self-conceptions, or mindset, and how people use them as a catalyst to structure themselves and their behaviors. She is an explorer of complex interpersonal processes.

First and foremost, *what is growth mindset?*

In her TEDx Talk called "The power of believing you can improve," she speaks about growth mindset and how it can exponentially change your life (2014). She speaks about a high school in Chicago, IL, where students received a grade of "not yet" rather than an "F," or failing grade. Dweck talks about experiences and research in her own life that correlate to the impact of this example. She poses the following questions:

- How are we raising our children?
- Are we raising our children for now instead of yet?

- Are we raising kids who are obsessed with getting A's?
- Are we raising kids who don't know how to dream big dreams?

Carol Dweck goes on to explain the importance of mindset and the vast impact it can make within our lives. By using the words "yet" or "not yet," it's found that children have greater confidence, giving them a path to create a more successful future. In one study she did, they found that every time they pushed children out of their comfort zone to learn something new or difficult, the neurons in their brain formed new, stronger connections (TED, 2014).

Carol stresses breaking free from the "tyranny of now" and rewarding the possibilities of "yet."

"Picture your brain forming new connections as you meet the challenge and learn. Keep on going."

—CAROL DWECK

As humans, our potential is infinite. I don't believe we have a destined, predetermined path designated to us in this life. That's why common terminology like "meant to be" or "supposed to be" are contradictory. Do we ever truly arrive anywhere? Or are we constantly in motion?

When we keep an open mind with a laser focus on growth and expansion, we feel more fulfilled. You have the ability to dig up your roots, plant new seeds and start over. It is never too late to grow or revise this version of yourself. You may not be where you want to be at this very moment, but you *will* get there… just not yet.

"Let us not be content to wait and see what will happen, but give us the determination to make the right things happen."

—PETER MARSHALL

CHASING YOUR FUTURE SELF: HOW TO STAY MOTIVATED

"The older you get, the more rules they're gonna try to get you to follow. You just gotta keep living, man."

—MATTHEW MCCONAUGHEY

Matthew McConaughey is a household name. He's an American, award-winning actor from Longview, TX. To think that we would have never been introduced to his talent if he'd continued down his original path toward becoming a lawyer is mind-blowing. McConaughey became a college graduate and got his first big break in *Dazed and Confused* in 1993 (Biography, 2020). By the 2000s, he had practically become "the king of romantic comedies." From *How to Lose A Guy in 10 Days* to *The Wedding Planner* and *Failure to Launch*, or even later hits like *Ghost of Girlfriends Past* and *Magic Mike*—Matthew McConaughey has a unique authenticity. He brings a part of his humor and charisma to each role he plays. He's also versatile. He's done everything from chick-flicks to biographical films. McConaughey didn't receive his first Oscar until 2014 for his movie *Dallas Buyers Club* (Biography, 2020). His acceptance speech for that well-deserved Oscar still circulates around the internet today due to its profound wisdom (Daily Motion, 2014).

Matthew discusses three things he needs each day:

1. Something to look up to
2. Something to look forward to
3. Something to chase

He looks up to God, he looks forward to his family, and he chases his hero. Who is his hero, though? He tells a story from when he was fifteen years old, and someone in his life asked him who his hero was. He, like any other teenager, didn't have an answer and needed to ponder on it. Two weeks later, this person asked him again. To which he answered, "it's me, in ten years." As he continued to get asked this question over the years, he realized that his hero would always be ten years away. He may never attain that version of self he chases, but it keeps him going. It keeps him striving for more.

When I first stumbled upon this speech, I watched it nearly ten times and sent it to half my contacts. I had never considered looking at motivation through such a lens, but when I took the time to reflect on my own motives and drives, I was no different from McConaughey. I've had people throughout my life that I'd admired, but I can't say I've had a defined "hero." There was never anyone's life I wanted. I just wanted to create a better one that uniquely suited me. It just hadn't dawned on me that I'd spent two decades chasing myself in circles.

"My life is the road, man. I need to keep moving."

—MATTHEW MCCONAUGHEY

CONSISTENCY IS KEY: THE POWER OF DAILY HABITS

"Past and Present I know well; each is a friend and sometimes an enemy to me. But it is the quiet, beckoning Future, an absolute stranger, with whom I have fallen madly in love."

—RICHELLE E. GOODIRCH

I have a question for you, reader. This one might require some brainpower.

Do you remember what your new year's resolution was this year?

Now, I don't ask this to make you feel bad about yourself. I ask because statistically, 45 percent of Americans make at least one resolution in January, yet only about 8 percent of people follow through with them (Lake, 2015). As the ball drops, fireworks erupt, and strangers embrace, it's easy to say you want to commit to change. However, will you actually commit? Will you choose to take action, be consistent, practice discipline, and keep yourself accountable?

Will you choose to chase the future version of yourself that you've been fantasizing about? I hope you choose to prove the statistics wrong.

In an article published by INC, Eric Holtzclaw discusses the power of consistency (2012). He explains that consistency allows for measurement and creates accountability. While he relates his findings to his professional pursuits, I believe consistency is essential in every area of our lives. We have to measure our growth, don't we? Establishing unique ways to measure our personal triumphs helps keep us accountable. It also makes the climb to our highest self feel more manageable.

"That's what it takes to get what you want. Not big scary leaps once a year. It takes small but irritating moves every single day."

—MEL ROBBINS

This year, Mel Robbins published her third best-selling book called *The High 5 Habit: Take Control of Your Life with One Simple Habit* (2021). In this, she reveals a habit she discovered amid the pandemic that has been transformative in her life. She got out of bed one morning, managed to look at her exhausted reflection, and as corny as it's going to sound—gave herself a high five. The next day, when she woke, she experienced something foreign, excitement to see herself. Mel Robbins takes a moment to be with herself, without judgment or criticism, each morning. Then, when she's energized herself with that intentional moment, she seals it with a high five to her reflection before she takes on the day ahead.

Ironically, I hadn't discovered Mel Robbins or her practices before writing this book. However, as someone who has consistently struggled with body image, I implemented a form of this habit years ago. Except, in true nature, I do it each night before bed.

Historically, my autoimmune condition has disrupted and frequently made me feel a loss of consistency in my life. One significant component is my body, and the other is my sleep, energy, and concentration. I've been taking baby steps to gain back that control for years through healthier lifestyle changes and small daily habits. There have been times when I've woken up and felt 20 pounds heavier, 0 percent rested, with hair falling into my hands. But there have also been days when I've woken up with that glowing face and "morning skinny" we all pray for. It's easy to compare one version of self to the other. For a while, I did. However, starting my day with judgment, shame, and guilt has never gotten me anywhere; it's only ever made matters worse. So, each night when I do my extensive skincare routine, I take one of Mel's intentional moments to show my self-love, acceptance, and appreciation for carrying me through each passing day. My body may not always work in my favor, but it's my lifeline; it's the vessel that shelters my worthiness. I give myself the strength, motivation, and courage to take on tomorrow with a simple smile at my own reflection.

ATOMIC HABITS: RECALIBRATING YOUR IDENTITY

"Habits are the compound interest of self-improvement."

—JAMES CLEAR

James Clear is an author of the NY Times bestseller, *Atomic Habits*. James is an expert in behavior change. His work has been utilized by teams in the NFL, NBA, and MLB (Rich Roll, 2018). If you're having trouble breaking old or counter-productive habits, I highly recommend you read his book.

While on a Podcast with Rich Roll in 2018, James Clear discusses overcoming habits, adopting better ones, and the internal processes behind habit making.

"Every action you take is a vote for the type of person you wish to become. No single instance will transform your beliefs, but as the votes build up, so does the evidence of your new identity."

—JAMES CLEAR

What I find most intriguing about James's research is a term he defines as "identity-based habits." He explains that our current behaviors are merely a reflection of our current identity, and if we want to change those habits, we must adopt a new identity. For instance, he explains, "the goal isn't to write a book, it's to *become* a writer" (Rich Roll, 2018). There's a difference between saying "I want this" and "*I am* this." Before we start goal-setting, we must decide who it is that we really want to be.

Be intentional with the habits you choose to inherit, for they become who we are.

"Don't judge each day by the harvest you reap but by the seeds that you plant."

—ROBERT LOUIS STEVENSON

THE NIGHT IS STILL YOUNG: PRACTICE PATIENCE, THERE'S A TIME FOR EVERYTHING

"Patience is bitter, but its fruit is sweet.

— JEAN-JACQUES ROUSSEAU

There are many misconceptions about personal growth and success in life. Finding your purpose, passions, and reason for being is simply the beginning of a journey. This is not a final destination but a pit stop in your very long voyage. You've taken the time to dive deep, confront the skeletons in your closet, and discover what motivates you to get out of bed each morning. However, once this is complete, another phase of your personal growth and development journey begins.

Simply identifying your purpose is not enough. You must chase it. This won't be a convenient mountain to climb; make no mistake. It very well may be the most challenging part of the journey. You must *choose* to wake up and *choose* yourself each day. You must choose to persevere regardless of what comes your way. You must practice consistency and self-regulation to achieve your wildest dreams. The effort required from you is extensive, but you're the only person in this world that can make it happen.

I've said it once, and I'm about to say it again. Transformation doesn't happen overnight. Striving to maintain our growth can often feel like tending to a garden. We plant seeds of change, and water with love and intention. Yet, we often wake up and feel the same. We don't notice differences or see our growth for weeks, months, and sometimes years. It's not easy to reprogram, transform, or uproot the identities within each of us.

Be patient and stay consistent, reader.

"In two weeks, you'll feel it. In four weeks, you'll see it. In eight weeks, you'll hear it."

—UNKNOWN

CHAPTER 11:

DON'T WORRY BABY

"Be happy for this moment. This moment is your life."

—OMAR KHAYYAM

I believe happiness exists in moments.

I want you to think about your favorite song and then ask yourself the following questions:

- How does it make you feel?
- What is it about this song that makes you feel this way?
- What else in your life gives you this type of feeling?

Can you tell I'm a music lover, readers?

What gave it away? Was it my whimsical yet oddly realistic viewpoint? Does my syntax tend to embody "la vie en rose" from time to time?

Maybe, but answer me this:

Isn't life more interesting with a badass soundtrack?

"Where words fail, music speaks."

—HANS CHRISTIAN ANDERSEN

Picking an all-time favorite song is a daunting task for me. However, I'd be lying to myself and all of you if I said there wasn't one particular song that comes to mind among my many favorites.

"Don't Worry Baby" by The Beach Boys may only be two minutes and forty-eight seconds long, but it never fails to bring a heart-warming smile to my face. That small fraction of time can completely transform my mood. With the sound of that first harmony, my spirit lifts. No matter the time, the day, or the place, it makes me want to dance my worries away. It instantly puts me at ease and in a happier mood. If this song doesn't make you want to dance around the kitchen, pretending a wooden spoon is your microphone—it's time to figure out what does provide you this type of bliss.

Maybe it's not music for you. Maybe it's nature. Maybe bearing witness to mother nature's beauty brings light into your world. Maybe you find joy in taking long walks, watching sunsets, climbing mountains, or exploring the great outdoors.

Maybe your happiness lies within human interaction. Perhaps little moments shared with your loved ones provide you with profound happiness. Whether it's a child, partner, parent, or friend, all of these moments are infinitely special. Maybe spending more time creating these precious moments with your loved ones makes you a happier human being.

Perhaps it's none of these things! If so, take the time to fully understand what makes you happy or makes your soul feel at peace.

"The present moment is filled with joy and happiness. If you are attentive, you will see it."

—THICH NHAT HANH

Happiness is readily available all around us at any given time, but only if we *choose* to see it. These precious moments within the present simply hold the opportunity to curate happiness. It's always within our reach. These little moments throughout our day feel magical because they are authentic, honest, and vulnerable. Moments aren't simply experienced. They're *felt*. When we choose to fully be in the present, we feel more happiness. If you can decipher what truly brings you joy, everything else makes a little more sense. When you do find these things, do them and do them often. The choice is up to you.

There are days that are going to be extremely difficult and maybe even devastating, but there's always at least one moment in the day that presents a silver lining, reminding you why you choose to get out of bed each morning. Remember that moment and let it be the light to guide you through your day.

THE PURSUIT OF HAPPINESS

"Happiness is a direction, not a place."

—SYDNEY J. HARRIS

Reader, I want you to use your imagination for a moment.

Imagine you're taking a trip; a much-needed vacation all by yourself, to any destination you wish.

Did your brain automatically picture a white sand beach, or did you imagine the journey to get to this tropical paradise?

My prediction is many of you immediately pictured a beach getaway with an extra-large piña colada. While that sounds glorious, what about all the moments leading up to that?

When I think about taking a vacation, every moment excites me. For as long as I can remember, I can never get a good night's sleep before a trip. I'm too damn giddy! The adrenaline and excitement running through my veins just walking through the terminal, planes taking off left and right, first-class people watching, the feeling of being thousands of feet up in the air... these are just a fraction of small moments that bring me happiness.

"The art of being happy lies in the power of extracting happiness from common things."

—HENRY WARD BEECHER

We often treat happiness like a destination rather than a direction.

Why though? Everything in life is about the journey rather than the destination, isn't it?

So, why do we wait to be happy? Why do we wait to find joy in moments?

Too many times, I hear the phrase, "*I'll be happy when...*"

When what?

- *When you lose weight?*
- *When you get that job?*
- *When you are in a relationship?*

This type of thinking is stealing your happiness on a daily basis. While you wait and obsess over everything you don't have, you're missing out on the beauty in everything you already have. As discussed earlier, isn't there happiness in moments every day if we choose to see them?

"The Constitution only gives people the right to pursue happiness. You have to catch it yourself."

—BENJAMIN FRANKLIN

SAM'S PHILOSOPHY FOR A HAPPY LIFE

"I believe that I can change the world. And as I'm striving to change the world, I will be happy."

—SAM BERNS

Progeria is a rare genetic disorder that affects nearly one in every four to eight million infants (Botelho, 2014). This approximates to only about 200 children worldwide. In an article by *Medical Daily*, Justin Caba explains that this rare condition, also known as Hutchinson-Gilford progeria syndrome, is caused by a mutation in our LMNA gene, which results in accelerated aging (2014).

Sam Berns was among that 200. In 2013, following his seventeenth birthday, he gave a TEDx Talk on happiness. Sam tells the story about his dream to play in his high school's marching band. However, due to his condition, he weighed only 50 pounds. Each snare drum and harness weighs nearly 40 pounds. Despite this disadvantage, he and his family worked with an engineer to design a harness that would accommodate for his weight or lack thereof. They finally produced a snare drum apparatus that weighed nearly 6 pounds and Sam was able to march with his peers like he'd always dreamed of.

"Happiness is a state of mind. It's just according to the way you look at things."

—WALT DISNEY

Sam developed his own philosophy to a happy life. This theory has three simple rules:

1. *Be okay* with what you ultimately can't do because there is so much you CAN do.
2. Surround yourself with people you want to be around.
3. Keep moving forward.

Bonus tip: Never miss a party if you can help it.

Unfortunately, Sam lost his battle to progeria a few short weeks after this inspirational TEDx Talk. However, his story and infectious spirit live on. Sam went to Foxborough High School, which happens to be in the hometown of the New England Patriots. The owner of the NFL team, Robert Kraft, had the chance to meet Sam. To which he said, Sam was a special young man whose inspirational story and positive outlook on life touched his heart, and that he felt richer for having known him (Botelho, 2014).

I believe we could all take a lesson out of Sam's playbook. Despite everything he had against him, he was unwilling to let it dictate his happiness.

"True happiness is to enjoy the present, without anxious dependence upon the future, not to amuse ourselves with either hopes or fears but to rest satisfied with what we have, which is sufficient, for he that is so wants nothing. The greatest blessings of mankind are within us and within our reach. A wise man is content with his lot, whatever it may be, without wishing for what he has not."

—SENECA

WHEN WILL YOU BE SATISFIED?

"The value of life lies not in the length of days, but in the use we make of them… Whether you find satisfaction in life depends not on your tale of years, but on your will."

—MICHEL DE MONTAIGNE

It's easy to pick apart anything in your life; dissecting beauty when something doesn't meet our initial expectations or standards. We're thrown off when real-life doesn't play out like it did in our heads. If not for self-awareness and self-monitoring our inner conscience, we can be the thief of our own happiness.

Courtney Ackerman explains that the concept of happiness and satisfaction are not the same and often get used interchangeably (2021). Rather than small moments of bliss, life satisfaction remains in evaluating one's life as a whole. To which I would pose, isn't that life made up of moments?

Therefore, if we make an effort to find joy, peace, and acceptance in life's precious moments, it just might equate to a satisfying life.

"Happiness is not a goal… it's a by-product of a life well lived."

—ELEANOR ROOSEVELT

CHAPTER 12:

EMBRACING YOUR JOURNEY AT EVERY PIT STOP

"Life is an opportunity, seize the day, live each day to the fullest. Life is not a project but a journey to be enjoyed."

—CATHERINE PULSIFER

As humans develop through the lifespan, there's room for continuous growth. From baby steps to graduations, we make way for new milestones at each pit stop. We are consistently met with greater heights to look forward to as we tread down this path of life. So, as you saunter through, I hope you choose to learn something new each day. I hope you decide to be curious, authentic, and courageous in your endeavors.

Lifelong learning can be defined as "the provision or use of both formal and informal learning opportunities throughout people's lives in order to foster the continuous development and improvement of the knowledge and skills needed for employment and personal fulfillment" (Collins English Dictionary, 2012).

But what does it mean to be a lifelong learner? What does lifelong learning look like?

A lifelong learner is an individual whose curiosity, knowledge, and depth of understanding see no bounds. A lifelong learner is an individual that is always seeking to grow, despite all they've mastered or accomplished. A lifelong learner is someone who makes strides each day to become a better, improved version of themselves.

"Those people who develop the ability to continuously acquire new and better forms of knowledge that they can apply to their work and to their lives will be the movers and shakers in our society for the indefinite future."

—CONFUCIUS

EARLY EFFORTS: MOLDING YOUNG MINDS

"At the end of the day, the most overwhelming key to a child's success is the positive involvement of parents.

JANE D. HULL

To all the momma and papa bears reading this,

Firstly, I salute you for your brave acts of service each day. Secondly, I'm not going to pretend like I know what it's like to fully walk in your shoes. Call me in ten years! However, within the perspective of growth, development, and lifelong learning, I feel it's important to address the influence and effect you have on young minds. Children most often learn by example. It's then our job as their wiser, larger humans to steer them in the right direction. It's our job to show them how it's done so that one day they're able to set a fine example.

"Are you the adult that you want your child to grow up to be?"

—BRENÉ BROWN

Adulting is hard, but being a parent is even harder. Parenting, in itself, is a full-time job. For any who may disagree with these statements, I'd challenge you not to only answer the question above but honestly evaluate how active you are in your child's personal growth and development. The responsibility and duty of a parent is to instill values and morals, teach discipline, as well as provide the love, understanding, and support your child so desperately needs. Just like everything else, there's no one-size-fits-all method to parenting. Every child is immensely different, requiring entirely different things.

While we attempt to meet their needs, make it a priority to lead by example. As educated, loving adults, we should be:

RAISING LIFELONG LEARNERS

Be the model of growth mindset for your young pupil. Instilling within them the power of yet, patience and perseverance are crucial to their development. Show them what it's like to be curious. Encourage them to ask questions!

RAISING INFORMED DREAMERS

Fostering young minds with imagination and creativity is just as important as informing of the harsh realities within the world we live in. Encourage your child to shoot for the moon but show them what is within their reach. Explore various avenues, and assist them in finding their route. The sky may be the limit, but nothing is going to come without effort and dedication. Informing our little dreamers about how the real world works prepares them to conquer with confidence.

RAISING CONFIDENT, EMPATHETIC CHILDREN

The golden rule isn't dead. Raise children who are comfortable standing in their vulnerability, owning their quirks, and supporting others. Show them different perspectives, slowly but surely teaching them how to walk in another's shoes. Most importantly, remind them of how capable they are. Create confident little healers.

And ultimately, remember that there's only so much you can do as their role model and biggest cheerleader. Sometimes you have to take the back seat and let your child learn for themselves.

"Parents can only give good advice or put them on the right paths, but the final forming of a person's character lies in their own hands."

—ANNE FRANK

COLLEGE AND EARLY ADULTHOOD: NAVIGATING THE CONFUSION

"No man should escape our universities without knowing how little he knows."

—J. ROBERT OPPENHEIMER

As mentioned prior, there are endless routes to success and happiness. Early adulthood can often feel like the blind leading the blind. You expect, hope, and dream it'll play out exactly as you've seen in your favorite rom-com... yet, it's increasingly less glamorous. As our brain finishes developing, our body changes, and every belief system we inhabit becomes questioned—you must learn to roll with the punches.

News flash—everyone around you is just as confused with what they're "supposed to be" doing.

EXPECT THE UNEXPECTED: SEARCHING FOR THE EYE OF THE STORM

I used to watch the *Wizard of Oz* on repeat growing up. It's a miracle I didn't burn through the VHS. From Judy Garland's angelic voice to her ruby red slippers, something resonated with me.

It's common when kids finally go off to college and discover "infinite freedom," they frequently over-indulge. Whether it be alcohol, drugs, or even sleep, we struggle to be our own parents when there's not someone constantly looking over our shoulders and accounting for our every move. For the delinquents who may be reading, you probably know where I'm going with this.

Once in a blue moon, you may find yourself a little too toasty coming back from that PIKE rager your classmate told you about. As you stumble back into your shoebox of a dorm room, the first and only thing you're going to want to do is lay on an elevated surface. Your feet just carried you all the way home, right? So they deserve to be put up? No. Chances are, if it felt like you floated home, the minute you put those feet up, I can guarantee the room will start spinning. The blissful feeling of resting your head goes from heavenly to "holy shit, bring me a garbage can" real quick. This, folks, is what I like to call *the Auntie Ems*.

However, this phenomenon doesn't just apply to stereotypical college partying; it applies to the trials and tribulations we encounter during that confusing period of life. The college experience is meant to test and challenge you. If nothing else, it's all one big exam to question who you really are as an individual. Some will come prepared, having memorized materials and recommended readings, and others will brave the unknown. Both of which are guaranteed to experience similar outcomes. At some point, you're going to feel like everything you are and ever known is up in the air. It's going to feel like you're stuck spinning in Auntie Em's farmhouse, with no clear end in sight. Fortunately, these experiences transform us and allow us to prepare for future scenarios. Just like the drunken one above, next time, you'll be ready with a hair tie, water, and a trash can. Or better yet, you'll remember what that tailspin felt like and be prepared to keep your feet on the ground, to stabilize until the storm passes.

Sometimes we have to simply wait for the twister to pass, while others, we must search for the eye of the storm. Search for clarity and peace within the technicolor chaos. Contrary to Glinda the Good Witch's advice, you don't have to take the yellow brick road to find your way home. Get creative. Did everyone else take note of the red brick road? Where did that lead? I suppose we'll never know.

The point is—there's an infinite amount of routes to your future self. Don't get stuck in thinking there's only one way to survive and thrive.

You've got time, kid—brave the storm.

"All you need is confidence in yourself. There is no living thing that is not afraid when it faces danger. True courage is in facing danger when you are afraid, and that kind of courage you have in plenty."

—L. FRANK BAUM, *THE WONDERFUL WIZARD OF OZ*

ADULTHOOD AND LATER LIFE: EMBRACING THE PRESENT AND LIVING FOR THE MOMENT

"Adults are just obsolete children and the hell with them."

—DR. SEUSS

As we develop and move into later adulthood, I feel this is a common attitude that's adopted. We feel we've lived enough life, accomplished enough, and can rest easy. I beg to differ, boomer!

Instead of each day passing into the next, take advantage of every moment. Keep learning new things, keep discovering joy in the little things, and keep growing. Growth doesn't have to hit a plateau once you're able to retire and collect social security. Find new hobbies, make new friends!

Just like every other developmental phase in life, adulthood and later life has an entirely new set of milestones, challenges, and benefits.

It's never too late to plant new seeds. What will you choose to learn today?

"Minds are like parachutes. They only function when they are open."

—JAMES DEWAR

AFTERWORD

———

"I don't know anything with certainty, but seeing the stars makes me dream."

—VINCENT VAN GOGH

Dearest Reader,

You've made it. My goal was never to change you, persuade you, or sell you on anything. I've never claimed to be an expert, just a passionate and thoughtful young lady. These words may be best-selling, they also may be trash. Despite my impending fate, I hope my words move you and make you question everything you've ever known.

The *Long Way Home* encompasses life and all the trials we endure within it as human beings. Just like your daily drive home, a road trip, or any grand voyage, taking your time to enjoy the process is necessary for our individual growth, peace of mind, and happiness. I wanted to provide others with a vantage point from which to view the world, giving you a tiny taste of the manipulation, delusion, and horse blinders society so sneakily tries to place on you. Only to reveal that you very well may be your own oppressor. The world often makes us feel small and unseen, but we have a choice in how that manifests itself. Our story doesn't have to fit in with every other superficial one on your Instagram feed or fulfill society's prophecy. For there is power and beauty in our vulnerabilities and differences.

If you learned nothing from reading my words:

You're the main character of your own story. It's uniquely yours. You hold the power and all the choices. You have so many resources at your fingertips. My research is telling of this. Your growth boils down to thoughts, decisions, and actions. What we think manifests itself as our reality. Choose your thoughts wisely.

My hope is that you choose transformation and authenticity and that you never stop learning or chasing a more enlightened version of self.

By unpacking, acknowledging, and understanding our flaws (whether societal or personal), we can collectively heal and move toward a better future. As individuals and a whole, we are capable of cohesion. We must confront conflict before we can see eye to eye, though.

Are you willing to put your ego aside for the greater good?

"Be the change that you wish to see in the world."

—MAHATMA GANDHI

xoxo,
R

ACKNOWLEDGMENTS

——

"Feeling gratitude and not expressing it is like wrapping a present and not giving it."

—WILLIAM ARTHUR WARD

Gratitude is something I like to exercise regularly. Therefore, I'd like to acknowledge those who have given this book and the stories within it, legs strong enough to move forward.

To New Degree Press, the Creator Institute, and my talented team of experts:

Eric Koester, Brian Bies, Regina Stribling, Mackenzie Joyce, Chuck Oexmann, Linda Berardelli, Leilla Summers, Venus Bradley, ChandaElaine Spurlock, Ty Mall, Natalie Bailey, Erica Fyffe, Ruslan Nabiev, Leah Pickett, as well as Gjorgji Pejkovski, Aleksandra Dabic, and the design team.

To early supporters and beta-readers:

Corrina Ardizzone, Liesl Babicka, James Beattie, Rita Beattie, Bari Watnick Brown, Chase Buckley, Cynthia Buckley, Ross

Buckley, Louise Bunker, Helen Cardaio, Lorrayne Carpenter, Denise Corsi, John Corsi, Ruth Del Vecchio, Chrisoula Devito, Michele Dibenedetto, Linda Dieffenbach, Drake Dole, Chris Gorogias, Elizabeth Gorogias, Gregory Gorogias, Mary Heagney, Madison Hernandez, Janet Hyde, Lindsey Jorgensen, Hanna Leigh Kelly, Mary Lee Kerr, Caitlin Kerrane, Daniel Kerrane, Jeffrey Kerrane, Irene Kisonas, John Kisonas, Antionette Klima, Cliff Klima, Sarah Leggio, Diane Maio, Danielle Mara, Jackson Martin, Allison Modano, Mike Modano, Mary Ann Mosier, Cameron Peters, Michael Riccobono, Steven Riccobono, Tina Riccobono, Natalia Rivera, Martha Roach, Heather Robinson, Taylor Salgado, Margaret Crean Tadeushuk, John Tarac, Christina Thiede, Ashton Thompson, Marina Unis, Maddie Voigt, James Cameron White, and John Zaharakis.

To my loving family:

Thomas Riccobono, Karen Kerrane Riccobono, and Matthew Riccobono.

You have all played differing roles in this process, but I'm incredibly thankful for your wisdom, creativity, support, and love.

Thank you for everything.

APPENDIX

INTRODUCTION:

Bellis, Mary. "Biography of Steve Jobs, Cofounder of Apple Computers." ThoughtCo. Last Modified July 3, 2019. Accessed September 15, 2021. https://www.thoughtco.com/steve-jobs-biography.

Biography. "F. Scott Fitzgerald." Last modified July 9, 2020. Accessed September 20, 2020. https://www.biography.com/writer/f-scott-fitzgerald.

Biography. "Jeff Bezos." Last modified February 2, 2021. Accessed October 23, 2020. https://www.biography.com/business-figure/jeff-bezos.

Mayo Clinic. "Hashimoto's Disease." Last Modified 2021. Accessed August 13, 2020. https://www.mayoclinic.org/diseases-conditions/hashimotos-disease/symptoms-causes/syc-20351855.

Stanford. "Tradition of Innovation: Larry Page and Sergey Brin, Cofounders." October 24, 2011. Video, 3:33. https://www.e.com/watch?v=x2WDVGodvnE.

Statista. "Leading e-commerce websites in the United States as of June 2021, based on number of monthly visits." Accessed Oct. 20, 2021. https://www.statista.com/statistics/271450/monthly-unique-visitors-to-us-retail-websites.

Statista. "Annual net revenue of Amazon from 2004 to 2020." Accessed on October 20, 2021. https://www.statista.com/statistics/266282/annual-net-revenue-of-amazoncom/

Statista. "Net revenue of Amazon from 1st quarter 2007 to 1st quarter 2021." Accessed October 20, 2021. https://www.statista.com/statistics/273963/quarterly-revenue-of-amazoncom.

CHAPTER 1:

Ascension Lutheran Church. "In Their Words: The Silent Generation (1929–1945)." December 26, 2018. Video, 14:31. https://www.youtube.com/watch?v=AQeBvPF5JVI.

Barge, Carlos. "What are the Characteristics of the Baby Boomer Generation?" Published October 23, 2019. Accessed September 11, 2020. https://www.bi.wygroup.net/customer-analytics/what-are-the-characteristics-of-the-baby-boomer-generation.

BuzzFeed Video. "Generations Throughout History." April 4, 2017. Video, 9:59. https://www.youtube.com/watch?v=IfYjGxI6AJ8

Dimock, Michael. "Defining Generations: Where Millennials End and Generation Z begins." Pew Research Center, January 17, 2019. Accessed October 2, 2021. https://www.pewresearch.org/fact-tank/2019/01/17/where-millennials-end-and-generation-z-begins/.

Fry, Richard, Ruth Iglielnik and Eileen Patten. "How Millennials Today Compare with Their Grandparents 50 Years Ago." Pew Research Center, March 16, 2018. Accessed September 12, 2020. https://www.pewresearch.org/fact-tank/2018/03/16/how-millennials-compare-with-their-grandparents.

Fry, Richard. "Millennials Are the Largest Generation in the US Labor Force." Pew Research Center, April 11, 2018. Accessed October 4, 2021. https://www.pewresearch.org/fact-tank/2018/04/11/millennials-largest-generation-us-labor-force.

FutureNow. "The Truth About Generation X." January 31, 2019. Video, 7:38. https://www.youtube.com/watch?v=pqwOEY6sR7I

Gross, David M. and Sophfronia Scott. "Living: Proceeding with Caution." TIME, July 16, 1990. http://content.time.com/time/subscriber/article/0,33009,970634,00.html

History. "Baby Boomers." A&E Television Networks, May 17, 2010. Last modified June 1, 2021. https://www.history.com/topics/1960s/baby-boomers-1.

History. "The Feminine Mystique by Betty Friedan Is Published." February 19, 1963. Accessed October 20, 2021. https://www.history.com/this-day-in-history/the-feminine-mystique-by-betty-friedan-is-published.

Hoffman, David. "Baby Boomers Speaking To Us From 1989." November 19, 2019. Video, 16:10. https://www.youtube.com/watch?v=_rTuPEdlhQs.

Howe, Neil. "The Silent Generation, The Lucky Few (Part 3 of 7)." *Forbes*, August 13, 2014. https://www.forbes.com/sites/neil-howe/2014/08/13/the-silent-generation-the-lucky-few-part-3-of-7.

Kurt, Daniel. "How the Financial Crisis Affected Millennials." Investopedia, July 20, 2020. Accessed October 15, 2021.

https://www.investopedia.com/insights/how-financial-crisis-affected-millennials/.

LifecourseCo. "Neil Howe & William Strauss discuss the Silent Generation on Underwood's Generations—2001." August 4, 2011. Video, 59:10. https://www.youtube.com/watch?v=L_owfM7CiCA.

Meola, Andrew. "Generation Z News: Latest characteristics, research, and facts." Insider Intelligence, July 29, 2021. Accessed October 21, 2021. https://www.insiderintelligence.com/insights/generation-z-facts.

NBC News. "Millennials: The Unluckiest Generation in Modern History?" July 2, 2020. Accessed May 9, 2021. https://www.youtube.com/watch?v=ikpoQfgxmkc.

Parker, Kim and Ruth Igielnik. "On the Cusp of Adulthood and Facing an Uncertain Future: What We Know About Gen Z So Far." Pew Research Center, 2020. Accessed October 21, 2021. https://www.pewresearch.org/social-trends/2020/05/14/on-the-cusp-of-adulthood-and-facing-an-uncertain-future-what-we-know-about-gen-z-so-far-2.

Pew Research Center. "Americans Name the Top Historic Events of Their Lifetimes," Published December 15, 2016. Accessed June 2,

2021. https://www.pewresearch.org/politics/2016/12/15/americans-name-the-top-historic-events-of-their-lifetimes/.

Pew Research Center. "Baby Boomers: The Gloomiest Generation." Published June 25, 2008. Accessed September 9, 2020. https://www.pewresearch.org/social-trends/2008/06/25/baby-boomers-the-gloomiest-generation.

Pew Research Center. "The Whys and Hows of Generations Research." Published September 3, 2015. Accessed September 10, 2020. https://www.pewresearch.org/politics/2015/09/03/the-whys-and-hows-of-generations-research.

Rothschild, Richard. "Silent Generation: A Voice in America." *Chicago Tribune*, March 28, 1999. Accessed October 8, 2021. https://www.chicagotribune.com/news/ct-xpm-1999-03-28-9903280125-story.html.

Ryback, Ralph. "From Baby Boomers to Generation Z," The Truisms of Wellness (blog). Psychology Today, February 22, 2016. https://www.psychologytoday.com/us/blog/the-truisms-wellness/201602/baby-boomers-generation-z.

Sanburn, Josh. "Millennials: The Next Greatest Generation?" TIME, May 9, 2013. Accessed October 13, 2021. https://nation.time.com/2013/05/09/millennials-the-next-greatest-generation/.

Statista Research Department. "US population by generation 2020." Last modified September 10, 2021. Accessed September 10, 2020. https://www.statista.com/statistics/797321/us-population-by-generation.

Stech, Ernie. "The Silent Generation." Emeritus College at ASU. Accessed September 4, 2021. https://emerituscollege.asu.edu/sites/default/files/ecdw/EVoice6/silent.html

TIME. "People: The Younger Generation." Published November 5, 1951. Accessed September 10, 2020. http://content.time.com/time/subscriber/article/0,33009,856950,00.html.

United States Census Bureau. "By 2030, All Baby Boomers Will Be Age 65 or Older." Published December 10, 2019. Accessed September 9, 2020. https://www.census.gov/library/stories/2019/12/by-2030-all-baby-boomers-will-be-age-65-or-older.html.

United States Census Bureau. "US and World Population Clock." Last modified October 7, 2021. Accessed September 10, 2020. https://www.census.gov/popclock.

Zogby, John. "The Baby Boomers' Legacy." *Forbes*, July 23, 2009. Accessed September 9, 2020. https://www.forbes.com/2009/07/22/baby-boomer-legacy-change-consumer-opinions-columnists-john-zogby.html?sh=584877394aco.

CHAPTER 2:

Abrams, Abigail. "Yes, Impostor Syndrome Is Real. Here's How to Deal With It." *TIME*, June 20, 2018. Accessed December 10, 2020. https://time.com/5312483/how-to-deal-with-impostor-syndrome.

Cherry, Kendra. "What Is Groupthink?" Verywell mind, November 12, 2020. Accessed October 2, 2021. https://www.verywellmind.com/what-is-groupthink-2795213.

The Center for Human Technology. 2021. https://www.humane-tech.com.

Netflix. *The Social Dilemma.* 2020. https://www.netflix.com/title/81254224

CHAPTER 3:

Barclay, Rachel. "Curiosity Changes the Brain to Boost Learning and Memory." Healthline, October 2, 2014. Accessed October 21. 2021. https://www.healthline.com/health-news/curiosity-boosts-learning-and-memory-10021.

Britannica. "Walt Disney." Last modified February 24, 2021. Accessed April 13, 2021. https://www.britannica.com/biography/Walt-Disney/additional-info#history.

Harrison, Spencer and Jon Cohen. "Curiosity Is Your Super Power." Filmed September 2018. TED video, 17:28. https://www.ted.com/talks/spencer_harrison_jon_cohen_curiosity_is_your_super_power

History. "Wright Brothers." Last modified November 13, 2020. Accessed December 20, 2020. https://www.history.com/topics/inventions/wright-brothers.

Smith, Adam. "6 Steps to Discover Your True Self." Published July 3, 2021. Accessed October 10, 2021. https://www.success.com/6-steps-to-discover-your-true-self.

Smithsonian National Air and Space Museum. "The Wright Brothers: Forefathers of Flight." 2021. https://airandspace.si.edu/exhibitions/wright-brothers/online/fly/1899/forefathers.cfm.

Statista. "Disney—statistics & facts." Last modified September 10, 2021. Accessed October 6, 2021. https://www.statista.com/topics/1824/disney/#dossierKeyfigures.

Borchers, Bob. TEDx Talks. "The Power of Curiosity. Filmed October 28, 2016 at TEDxAmadorValleyHigh.". Video, 13:56. https://www.youtube.com/watch?v=FRiEJIEbTD0

University of St. Augustine. "55+ Self-Discovery Questions for Personal Growth." Published April 2020. Accessed October 20, 2021. https://www.usa.edu/blog/self-discovery-questions.

CHAPTER 4:

Centers for Disease Control and Prevention. "Why It Matters | Nutrition | CDC." Last modified January 25, 2021. Accessed October 15, 2021. https://www.cdc.gov/nutrition/about-nutrition/why-it-matters.html.

Escalante, Jeff. "Basic Needs." Medium, December 11, 2015. Accessed October 15, 2021. https://medium.com/pragmatic-life/basic-needs-b08130301d27.

Gunnars, Kris. "28 Health And Nutrition Tips That Are Actually Evidence-Based." Last modified July 2, 2021. Accessed October 12, 2021. https://www.healthline.com/nutrition/27-health-and-nutrition-tips#TOC_TITLE_HDR_5.

Harvard Medical School. "How Much Sleep Do We Really Need?" Published August 1, 2019. Accessed December 10, 2020. https://www.health.harvard.edu/staying-healthy/how-much-sleep-do-we-really-need.

Homeless Hub. "Maslow's Hierarchy of Needs." 2021. https://www.homelesshub.ca/toolkit/maslows-hierarchy-needs

Mayo Clinic. "Exercise: 7 benefits of regular physical activity." Last modified October 8, 2021. Accessed October 20, 2021. https://www.mayoclinic.org/healthy-lifestyle/fitness/in-depth/exercise/art-20048389.

Mayo Clinic. "How many hours of sleep are enough?" Last modified May 15, 2021. Accessed December 13, 2020. https://www.mayoclinic.org/healthy-lifestyle/adult-health/expert-answers/how-many-hours-of-sleep-are-enough/faq-20057898.

Mayo Clinic. "Water: How much should you drink every day?" Last modified October 14, 2020. Accessed October 4, 2021. https://www.mayoclinic.org/healthy-lifestyle/nutrition-and-healthy-eating/in-depth/water/art-20044256.

ProHealth Care. "ProHealth Minute: Importance of Nutrition." March 25, 2017. Video, 1:01. https://www.youtube.com/watch?v=ohEOBnWtXCc%5C.

United States Interagency Council on Homelessness. "Arizona Homelessness Statistics." 2020. https://www.usich.gov/homelessness-statistics/az.

Watson, Stephanie and Kristeen Cherney. "The Effects of Sleep Deprivation on Your Body." Healthline, May 15, 2020. Accessed May 13, 2021. https://www.healthline.com/health/sleep-deprivation/effects-on-body.

World Health Organization. "Sexual and Reproductive Health." 2021. https://www.who.int/teams/sexual-and-reproductive-health-and-research-(srh)/areas-of-work/sexual-health.

CHAPTER 5:

Benincasa, Sara. "Psychologists Say Single People Are More Fulfilled. I'm Getting to Understand Why." *The Guardian*, August 10, 2016. Accessed October 11, 2020. https://www.theguardian.com/commentisfree/2016/aug/10/psychology-single-people-more-fulfilled-relationships

Brenner, Abigail. "7 Tips to Create Healthy Boundaries with Others," In Flux (blog). Psychology Today, November 21, 2015. Accessed October 5, 2021. https://www.psychologytoday.com/us/blog/in-flux/201511/7-tips-create-healthy-boundaries-others.

Brodwin, Erin. "It's Better to Be Single, According to Science." *Business Insider*, February 13, 2018. Accessed October 12, 2020. https://thriveglobal.com/stories/it-s-better-to-be-single-according-to-science.

Cannon, Joanna. "We All Want to Fit In," Brainstorm (blog). *Psychology Today*, July 13, 2016. Accessed October 9, 2021. https://www.psychologytoday.com/us/blog/brainstorm/201607/we-all-want-fit-in.

Chatel, Amanda. "13 Things To Do When You're Single and Not Dating." *Bustle*, December 14, 2015. Accessed October 10, 2020. https://www.bustle.com/articles/129223-13-things-to-do-when-youre-single-and-not-dating-anyone

Cherry, Kendra. "How Social Support Contributes to Psychological Health." Verywell Mind, April 14, 2020. Accessed on October 11, 2021. https://www.verywellmind.com/social-support-for-psychological-health-4119970

Chesak, Jennifer. "The No BS Guide to Protecting Your Emotional Space." *Healthline*, December 10, 2018. Accessed October 9, 2020. https://www.healthline.com/health/mental-health/set-boundaries#boundary-basics-and-benefits.

Cigna: Loneliness and the Workplace, 2020 US Report.

https://www.cigna.com/static/www-cigna-com/docs/about-us/newsroom/studies-and-reports/combating-loneliness/cigna-2020-loneliness-report.pdf.

Cosmopolitan. "The Fun Things Everyone Should Do When They're Single." Published January 8, 2020. Accessed January 20, 2020. https://www.cosmopolitan.com/uk/love-sex/relationships/a30439422/things-to-do-single/

DePaulo, Bella. "What Does 'Single' Mean?" Living Single (blog). *Psychology Today*, April 3, 2011. https://www.psychologytoday.com/us/blog/living-single/201104/what-does-single-mean

Formica, Michael J. "Ten Elements of Effective Relationships," Enlightened Living (blog). *Psychology Today*, January 20, 2010. Accessed October 20, 2020. https://www.psychologytoday.com/us/blog/enlightened-living/201001/ten-elements-effective-relationships.

Jalili, Candice. "9 Ways Being Single Can Improve Your Life." *TIME*, September 20, 2018. Accessed October 12, 2020. https://time.com/5401028/benefits-being-single-experts.

Kravitz, Jamie. "5 Wise Pieces of Expert Advice to Remember If You've Been Single Forever." *Elite Daily*, February 14, 2018. Accessed October 2, 2021. https://www.elitedaily.com/p/this-advice-for-single-people-from-dating-experts-is-actually-really-useful-8140749.

Morin, Amy. "Depression Statistics Everyone Should Know." Verywell Mind, May 11, 2021. https://www.verywellmind.com/depression-statistics-everyone-should-know-4159056

TEDx Talks. "What no one ever told you about people who are single." May 11, 2017. Video, 18:00. https://www.youtube.com/watch?v=lyZysfafOAs

World Health Organization. "Depression." WHO, September 13, 2021. Accessed October 13, 2021. https://www.who.int/news-room/fact-sheets/detail/depression.

Mental Health Foundation. "Mental health statistics: relationships and community." Last modified 2021. Accessed October 15, 2021. https://www.mentalhealth.org.uk/statistics/mental-health-statistics-relationships-and-community.

CHAPTER 6:

American Museum of Natural History. "Science Bulletins: Brains Change with Trauma." June 25, 2012. Video, 2:07. https://www.youtube.com/watch?v=X40-EXLkA7Y.

American Psychological Association. "Trauma." Last modified 2021. https://www.apa.org/topics/trauma.

American Psychiatric Association. "What Are Dissociative Disorders?" August 2018. https://www.psychiatry.org/patients-families/dissociative-disorders/what-are-dissociative-disorders

Biography. "Audrey Hepburn: Film and Fashion Icon," December 6, 2020. Video, 44:58. https://www.youtube.com/watch?v=thRD7XVy_Xs.

Bremner, J. Douglas. "Traumatic Stress: Effects on the Brain." *Dialogues in clinical neuroscience* vol. 8,4 (2006): 445-61. https://doi.org/10.31887/DCNS.2006.8.4/jbremner

Britannica. "Hippocampus." https://www.britannica.com/science/hippocampus

Cherry, Kendra. "What Is The Hippocampus." Verywell Mind, July 22, 2020. Accessed June 20, 2021. https://www.verywellmind.com/what-is-the-hippocampus-2795231.

Dobric, Mirjana. "32+ Upsetting and Interesting Facts About PTSD for 2021." LoudCloud Health, January 28, 2021. Accessed October 11, 2021. https://loudcloudhealth.com/resources/ptsd-statistics/.

Doctor Oz. "Oprah Winfrey Opens Up About Childhood Trauma in Her Past." April 30, 2021. Video, 12:46. https://www.youtube.com/watch?v=kEzGN39duWg.

Mayo Clinic. "Chronic stress puts your health at risk." Last modified July 8, 2021. Accessed May 9, 2021. https://www.mayoclinic.

org/healthy-lifestyle/stress-management/in-depth/stress/art-20046037

Psych2Go. "5 Types of Unhealed Trauma." August 13, 2020. Video, 3:34. https://www.youtube.com/watch?v=GCeLbvEw_8w.

Sidran Institute: Traumatic Stress Disorder Fact Sheet, 2018. https://www.sidran.org/wp-content/uploads/2018/11/Post-Traumatic-Stress-Disorder-Fact-Sheet-.pdf.

Kipp, Mastin. TEDx Talks. "United States of Differentiation." April 29, 2019. Video, 21:02. https://www.youtube.com/watch?v=bC-mi1Ghoack.

The American Institute of Stress. "How Fight or Flight Response Works." 2020. https://www.stress.org/how-the-fight-or-flight-response-works.

The National Council for Behavioral Health: How to Manage Trauma. (US, 2020). https://www.thenationalcouncil.org/wp-content/uploads/2013/05/Trauma-infographic.pdf?daf=375ateTbd56.

Tull, Matthew. "Why People with PTSD Use Emotional Avoidance to Cope." Verywell Mind, March 24, 2020. Accessed October 10, 2021. https://www.verywellmind.com/ptsd-and-emotional-avoidance-2797640.

CHAPTER 7:

Barth, F. Diane. "5 Ways to Find Balance in Your Life," *Off the Couch* (blog). Psychology Today, September 21, 2014. https://www.

psychologytoday.com/us/blog/the-couch/201409/5-ways-find-balance-in-your-life.

Gilbert, Elizabeth. "Bio." Last modified 2021. Accessed September 12, 2020. https://www.elizabethgilbert.com/bio.

Gilbert, Elizabeth. "It's OK to Feel Overwhelmed. Here's What to Do Next." Filmed virtually on April 2, 2020. TED video, 1:02:11. https://www.ted.com/talks/elizabeth_gilbert_it_s_ok_to_feel_overwhelmed_here_s_what_to_do_next/up-next.

Harvard Medical School. "How much sleep do we really need?" *Harvard Health Publishing*, August 1, 2019. https://www.health.harvard.edu/staying-healthy/how-much-sleep-do-we-really-need.

National Counseling Society. "How your environment affects your mental health." Last modified 2021. Accessed September 25, 2020. https://nationalcounsellingsociety.org/blog/posts/how-your-environment-affects-your-mental-health

Olson, Eric J. "How many hours of sleep are enough for good health?" Mayo Clinic. Accessed September 9, 2020. https://www.mayoclinic.org/healthy-lifestyle/adult-health/expert-answers/how-many-hours-of-sleep-are-enough/faq-20057898.

Rampton, John. "Manipulate Time with These Powerful Twenty Time Management Tips." *Forbes*, May 1, 2018. https://www.forbes.com/sites/johnrampton/2018/05/01/manipulate-time-with-these-powerful-20-time-management-tips/?sh=3c5c4c1c57ab

Scott, Elizabeth. "The Toxic Effects of Negative Self-Talk." Verywell Mind. Last modified February 25, 2020. https://www.verywellmind.com/negative-self-talk-and-how-it-affects-us-4161304.

Simone, Fran. "Negative Self-Talk: Don't Let It Overwhelm You," A Family Affair (blog). *Psychology Today*, December 4, 2017. https://www.psychologytoday.com/us/blog/family-affair/201712.

Sunl, Eric. "How Much Sleep Do We Really Need?" *Sleep Foundation*. Last modified March 10, 2021. Accessed September 10, 2020. https://www.sleepfoundation.org/how-sleep-works/how-much-sleep-do-we-really-need.

Watson, Stephanie and Kristeen Cherney. "The Effects of Sleep Deprivation on Your Body." *Healthline*, May 15, 2020. https://www.healthline.com/health/sleep-deprivation/effects-on-body.

CHAPTER 8:

Biographics. "Vincent Van Gogh: The Humble Genius." January 10, 2020. Video, 20:22. https://www.youtube.com/watch?v=wI2i-5ca1RT4.

Biography. "Vincent van Gogh." Last modified March 4, 2020. Accessed on October 4, 2021. https://www.biography.com/artist/vincent-van-gogh.

Brown, Brené. "The Power of Vulnerability." Filmed June 2010 in Houston, TX. TED video, https://www.ted.com/talks/brene_brown_the_power_of_vulnerability?language=en#t-309812.

Brown, Brené. "Media Contact & Press Kit." 2021. https://brene-brown.com/media-kit/.

Do Something. "11 Facts About Teens and Self-Esteem." https://www.dosomething.org/us/facts/11-facts-about-teens-and-self-esteem#fn10

Paintonia. "How Much Is The Starry Night Worth? (Van Gogh)." Accessed Oct. 20, 2021. https://paintona.com/how-much-is-the-starry-night-worth/.

Reitman, Catherine. "A Guide to Believing in Yourself (But for Real This Time)." TEDxToronto." December 1, 2017. Video, 13:13. https://www.youtube.com/watch?v=jpRqbP9Nv9.

Ware, Bronnie. "Regrets of Dying." https://bronnieware.com/blog/regrets-of-the-dying/

CHAPTER 9:

Academy of Ideas. "Viktor Frankl: Logotherapy and Man's Search for Meaning." July 26, 2016. Video, 6:46.

https://www.youtube.com/watch?v=okJ3KQ4S-ts&t=200s.

Acceptance Rate. "Harvard University." Accessed October 3, 2021. https://www.acceptancerate.com/schools/harvard-university

Britannica. "Viktor Frankl." https://www.britannica.com/biography/Viktor-Frankl

Cuncic, Arlin. "What is Logotherapy?" Verywell Mind, July 8, 2021. Accessed August 21, 2021. https://www.verywellmind.com/an-overview-of-victor-frankl-s-logotherapy-4159308.

Koester, Eric. "What Is The Right Mindset to Write a Book." November 6, 2019. Video, 4:24. https://www.youtube.com/watch?v=O5yipKUPfjg.

Improvement Pill. "The Japanese Formula for Happiness—Ikigai." January 13, 2019. Video, 6:45. https://www.huffpost.com/entry/our-cry-for-meaning-aggre_b_139984.

McLeod, Nia Simone. "Viktor Frankl Quotes on Life, Suffering, and Success." Everyday Power, June 10, 2021. Accessed October 13, 2021. https://everydaypower.com/viktor-frankl-quotes.

Mitsuhashi, Yukari. "Ikigai: A Japanese concept to improve work and life." BBC, August 7, 2017. Accessed October 16, 2020. https://www.bbc.com/worklife/article/20170807-ikigai-a-japanese-concept-to-improve-work-and-life.

Mogi, Ken. "This Japanese secret to a longer and happier life is gaining attention from millions around the world." CNBC, May 22, 2019. Accessed October 14, 2020. https://www.cnbc.com/2019/05/22/the-japanese-secret-to-a-longer-and-happier-life-is-gaining-attention-from-millions.html.

Pattakos, Alex. "Our Cry For Meaning: Aggression, Addition, Depression." HuffPost, December 6, 2008. Last modified November 27, 2011. https://www.huffpost.com/entry/our-cry-for-meaning-aggre_b_139984.

Tamashiro, Tim official website. "Biography." Accessed Oct. 20, 2021. http://www.timtamashiro.ca/tim-tamashiro-bio

Tamashiro, Tim. TEDx Talks. "How to Ikigai TEDxYYC." September 8, 2019. Video, 12:42. https://www.youtube.com/watch?v=pk-Pc-JS2QaU.

Bidle, Emily. TEDx Talks. "Ikigai: The Secret to a Purposeful Life. | TEDxYouth@ASIJ." March 14, 2019. Video, 9:44. https://www.youtube.com/watch?v=SDbYVlJntYU.

Wolters Kluwer Health: Lippincott Williams and Wilkins. "Sense of purpose in life linked to lower mortality and cardiovascular risk." Dec. 3, 2015. https://www.sciencedaily.com/releases/2015/12/151203112844.htm

CHAPTER 10:

Biography. "Matthew McConaughey." Last modified August 31, 2020. Accessed September 3. 2021. https://www.biography.com/actor/matthew-mcconaughey.

Daily Motion. "Matthew McConaughey—Acceptance Speech Oscars 2014. https://www.dailymotion.com/video/x1ec340

Dweck, Carol. "The Power of believing that you can improve." Filmed November 2014 in Norrkoping, Sweden. TED video, 10:11. https://www.ted.com/talks/carol_dweck_the_power_of_believing_that_you_can_improve/up-next?language=en.

Holtzclaw, Eric. "Power of Consistency: 5 Rules." *Inc.*, June 12. 2012. https://www.inc.com/eric-v-holtzclaw/consistency-power-success-rules.html

Lake, Rebecca. "New Year's Resolution Statistics:23 Facts to Keep." Last modified November 16, 2015. Accessed October 10, 2021. https://www.creditdonkey.com/new-years-resolution-statistics.html.

Rich Roll. "How To Build Awesome Habits: James Clear, Rich Roll Podcast." October 28, 2018. Video, 2:09:25. https://www.youtube.com/watch?v=s9uDVVWN_ZE

Robbins, Mel. *The High 5 Habit: Take Control of Your Life with One Simple Habit.* Hay House Inc., 2021.

TED. "Carol Dweck | Speaker." 2021. https://www.ted.com/speakers/carol_dweck

Robbins, Mel. TEDx Talks. "How to Stop Screwing Yourself Over. TEDxSF." June 11, 2011. Video, 21:39. https://www.youtube.com/watch?v=Lp7E973z0zc

CHAPTER 11:

Ackerman, Courtney E. "Life Satisfaction: Theory and Four Contributing Factors." Last modified November 3, 2021. Accessed on May 4, 2020. https://positivepsychology.com/life-satisfaction/.

Botelho, Greg. "Beloved teen Sam Berns dies at 17 after suffering from rare disease." CNN, January 12, 2014. Accessed April 13, 2020. https://www.cnn.com/2014/01/11/us/progeria-sam-berns-dies/index.html.

Caba, Justin. "Teen With Progeria, Sam Berns, Dies; Parents Continue Search For Answers To Rare, Genetic Disease." Medical Daily, January 13, 2014. Accessed April 13, 2020. https://www.medicaldaily.com/teen-progeria-sam-berns-dies-parents-continue-search-answers-rare-genetic-disease-266967.

Berns, Sam. TEDx Talks. "My philosophy for a happy life. TEDx-MidAtlantic." December 13, 2013. Video, 12:45. https://www.youtube.com/watch?v=36m10-tM05g.